Hwlffordd

Haverfordwest

MEWN HEN LUNIAU
IN OLD PHOTOGRAPHS

Tŷ o'r canol oesoedd, yn bennaf, yn Stryd y Santes Fair yn yr 1880au – y tŷ hynaf yn ôl pob sôn yn Hwlffordd yr adeg honno. Mae'n rhaid bod y llun hwn wedi'i dynnu ychydig cyn dymchwel y ddau dŷ. Codwyd y Neuadd Ddirwest a Siambr y Cyngor ar y safle yn ddiweddarach.

A largely medieval house in St. Mary's Street in the 1880s, reputedly then the oldest house in Haverfordwest. This must have been taken shortly before both the houses were demolished. The Temperance Hall and Council Chamber were built on the site.

Hwlffordd

Haverfordwest

MEWN HEN LUNIAU
IN OLD PHOTOGRAPHS

Casglwyd Gan Yr
ADRAN GWASANAETHAU DIWYLLIANNOLL DYFED
Collected by
DYFED CULTURAL SERVICES DEPARTMENT

Alan Sutton Publishing Limited
Phoenix Mill · Far Thrupp
Stroud · Gloucestershire

Cyhoeddwyd ar y cyd â
Published in collaboration with

**Adran Gwasanaethau Diwylliannol
Cultural Services Department**
CYNGOR SIR
DYFED
COUNTY COUNCIL

Cyhoeddwyd gyntaf ym 1992
First published 1992

Manylion catalogio y Llyfrgell Brydeinig
British Library Cataloguing in Publication Data

Dyfed Cultural Services Department
  Haverfordwest in Old Photographs
  I. Title
  942.96

ISBN 0-86299-804-2

Typeset in Sabon 9/10
Cysodi a gwaith gwreiddiol gan
Typesetting and origination by
Alan Sutton Publishing Limited.
Argraffwyd ym Mhrydain Fawr gan
Printed in Great Britain by
The Bath Press, Avon.

Clawr: Hwlffordd o'r gogledd, 1884, gyda'r castell a'r carchar ar y chwith, Eglwys San
Martin ar y dde, gyda phladurwyr yn lladd gwair ym mhen blaen y llun.
Cover: Haverfordwest from the north, 1884, with the castle and prison on the left,
St. Martin's Church on the right and mowing in the foreground.

Y Cynnwys • Contents

Cyflwyniad
Introduction   7

1. *Golygfeydd o'r Strydoedd*
   Street Scenes   11

2. *Glannau'r Afon*
   The Riverside   41

3. *Achlysuron Arbennig*
   Special Events   49

4. *Masnach*
   Commerce   65

5. *Trafnidiaeth*
   Transport   83

6. *Sefydliadau*
   Institutions   93

7. *Adeiladau Crefyddol*
   Religious Buildings   115

8. *Hamddena*
   Recreation   127

9. *Adeiladau Nodedig*
   Notable Houses   149

Diolchiadau
Acknowledgements   160

Scotchwell, yn gynnar yn yr ugeinfed ganrif.
Scotchwell, early twentieth century.

Dymchwel yr hen Farchnad Bysgod ger Eglwys y Santes Fair, 1950au.
The old Fish Market by St. Mary's Church being dismantled, 1950s.

Cyflwyniad

Mae tref Hwlffordd wedi'i lleoli ar Afon Cleddau Wen mewn man lle roedd modd rhydio'r afon ac a oedd yn gyfleus hefyd i'r fasnach forwrol, yr oedd ffyniant y dref yn dibynnu arni i raddau helaeth iawn.

Mae bywyd y dref fach fywiog hon ar y bryn, a fu'n ganolfan i'r gymuned amaethyddol ac i'r gymuned forwrol, yn cael ei gyfleu yma drwy gyfrwng lluniau o gasgliadau'r llyfrgell, yr amgueddfa a'r archifdy a weinyddir gan Gyngor Sir Dyfed yn Sir Benfro. Neilltuir penodau am ei hanes masnachol a diwydiannol, am ei strydoedd ac am y rhannau hynny o'r dref sydd ger yr afon, am ddathliadau ac am hamddena yn y dref ac am ei sefydliadau, yn ogystal ag am rai o gartrefi'r gwyr mawr yn y dref a gerllaw.

Codwyd y castell gan Tancard, un o'r fflemingiaid, yn gynnar yn y ddeuddegfed ganrif, a daeth i feddiant gwŷr adnabyddus dros y canrifoedd gan gynnwys y Brenin ac Eleanor o Castille. Yn 1220 anrheithiwyd y dref, oedd wedi datblygu o amgylch y castell, hyd at furiau'r castell gan Llywelyn ap Iorwerth. Bu lluoedd oedd yn deyrngar i Owain Glyn Dŵr yn gwarchae'r castell yn 1405, ond parhaodd y castell yn gyfan tan 1648 pan gafodd ei ddinistrio'n rhannol ar orchymyn Cromwell, gan ei adael yn adfail fel y'i gwelir heddiw.

Roedd Hwlffordd yn un o drefi mwyaf Cymru yn y canol oesoedd gyda'i phriordy cyfoethog, oedd ym meddiant y canoniaid Awstinaidd ynghyd â thy'r brodyr Dominicaidd. Ffynnai ar fasnach ar hyd yr arfordir ac â gwledydd tramor, gan elwa ar y breintiau hael a roddwyd i fwrdeisiaid y dref. Tyfodd y dref lan y rhiw i gynnwys y tir o amgylch Eglwys y Santes Fair, canolbwynt un o'r tri phlwyf yn y brif dref; llewyrchai'r farchnad ac erbyn yr unfed ganrif ar bymtheg roedd y dref yn anfon ei haelod seneddol ei hunan i'r Senedd. O'r cyfnod hwn ymlaen gallai dinasyddion y dref fanteisio hefyd ar welliannau i'r dref, y talwyd amdanynt o'r rhenti a'r elw a geid o diroedd a thai a roddwyd gan Syr John Perrot, a oedd yn gymeriad tra lliwgar.

Trawodd y pla du y dref yn 1651, a bu farw cannoedd lawer o bobl, gan achosi dioddefaint mawr yn y dref. Ni welwyd y dref yn llewyrchu drachefn tan y ddeunawfed ganrif, pryd y daeth yn ffasiynol i'r gwŷr mawr godi tai yn y trefi, yn ychwanegol at eu hystadau mawr yn y wlad, gan gefnogi sefydliadau a ddarparai adloniant yn ystod y gaeaf.

Er bod llawer o gynllun y strydoedd yn y canol oesoedd yn parhau hyd heddiw, mae'r rhan fwyaf o'r adeiladau yn dyddio o'r ddeunawfed ganrif a'r bedwaredd ganrif ar bymtheg, o leiaf yn eu gwedd allanol. Y sylfaen i batrwm y strydoedd oedd y mannau lle gellid croesi'r afon. Codwyd yr Hen Bont, ar safle pont ganoloesol, gan Syr John Philipps o Bictwn yn 1726. Dros ganrif yn ddiweddarach, yn 1837, codwyd y Bont Newydd gan roi ffordd well i mewn i'r dref ar hyd terasau ysblennydd Maes Victoria, a godwyd yn lle'r strydoedd canoloesol oedd yn mynd â'u pen iddynt. Y gŵr allweddol yn y datblygiad hwn oedd pensaer lleol a gŵr busnes blaenllaw, William Owen; ac aeth mor bell â thalu am y bont â'r arian ei hunan. Roedd gwelliannau dinesig eraill yn y bedwaredd ganrif ar bymtheg yn cynnwys Neuadd y Sir a'r Farchnad Grawn, a gynlluniwyd gan William Owen, y Carchar ger y Castell, y Wyrcws ar Riw'r Prior, a'r Ysbyty ar Grîn Tomos Sant. Cafodd llawer o'r capeli anghydffurfiol ysblennydd eu codi yn y cyfnod hwn hefyd. Fel y dengys y lluniau, byddai'r strydoedd llydan newydd yn gefndir heb eu hail i'r gorymdeithiau a'r dathliadau niferus.

Cyrhaeddodd y rheilffordd y dref yn 1853, a lleihaodd y fasnach forwrol yn sydyn o ganlyniad i hynny, gan gyfrannu at ddirywiad y rhannau hynny o'r dref oedd gerllaw'r afon, er bod y rheilffordd o fantais i fusnesau megis gwaith buddeiau y teulu Llewellin, a allai werthu eu nwyddau i farchnad ehangach. Parhaodd y dref yn ganolfan i'r gymuned amaethyddol, a Hwlffordd oedd prif dref Sir Benfro tan ad-drefnu llywodraeth leol yn 1974. Bu'n ganolfan siopa o bwys ers blynyddoedd mawr. O'r 1860au ymlaen Commerce House yn Stryd y Farchnad oedd un o siopau adrannol mwyaf Cymru, tra mae siop adrannol Ocky White yn un o'r lliaws o fusnesau llwyddiannus a sefydlwyd yn ddiweddarach. Erbyn heddiw ceir yno archfarchnadoedd mawr, fel sy'n wir am bobman.

Mae'r ardal ger yr afon wedi'i bywiogi unwaith eto. Mae gwelliannau i'r ffyrdd, a chanolfan siopa newydd, yn denu ymwelwyr i'r dref, sydd hefyd yn tyfu fel canolfan i grwydro Gorllewin Cymru. Dymchwelwyd rhai o hen adeiladau diddorol y dref ond y gobaith yw y bydd y lluniau hyn yn helpu i gadw treftadaeth yr hen gymuned hon sydd yn dirwyn yn ôl am ganrifoedd.

Pysgotwraig o Langwm y tu allan i Eglwys y Santes Fair, tua 1905. Arferai'r menywod hyn gerdded cryn bellter i werthu eu pysgod cregyn.
A Llangwm fisherwoman outside St. Mary's Church, c1905. These women walked long distances to sell their shellfish.

Introduction

The town of Haverfordwest is situated on the Western Cleddau at a point where it has been both fordable and accessible to the sea-going trade, upon which much of its fortune has depended.

The life of this bustling, hilly town, centre of a rural and maritime community, is depicted here in photographs from the collections of the library, museum and record office administered by Dyfed County Council in the Pembrokeshire area. There are chapters devoted to its trade and industry, streets and riverside, celebrations, recreation and institutions, and to some grander houses in and around the town.

The castle was established by Tancard, a Fleming, in the early twelfth century and, over the centuries, it was in the possession of notable people, including the sovereign and Eleanor of Castile. In 1220 the town, which had developed around the castle, was burnt up to the castle walls by Llewellyn ap Iorwerth. The castle was besieged in 1405 by forces loyal to Owain Glyndwr, but it was not until 1648 that it was partially destroyed on the orders of Cromwell, leaving the ruins much as we see them today.

The medieval town, one of the largest in Wales, with its wealthy priory of Augustinian canons and a Dominican friary, thrived on its coastal and foreign trade and benefited from generous privileges granted to the burgesses of the town. Spreading up the hill to the area around St. Mary's Church, centre of one of the three parishes in the main town, its markets flourished and, by the sixteenth century, it was sending its own member to Parliament. From that time its citizens also benefited from town improvements paid for from rents and profits from land and houses granted by the colourful Sir John Perrot.

Plague struck in 1651, when several hundred people died, reducing the town to great distress. It was not until the eighteenth century that it began to regain its prosperity, when it became fashionable for country landowners to build town houses and support places for winter entertainments.

Although much of the medieval street plan remains today, most buildings are predominantly of the eighteenth and nineteenth centuries, at least in outward appearance. River crossings have determined the layout of streets. The Old Bridge was built on the site of a medieval bridge by Sir John Philipps of Picton in 1726. Over a century later, in 1837, the New Bridge provided an improved approach to the town via the fine terraces of Victoria Place, which replaced crumbling medieval streets. Prominent local architect and businessman William Owen was instrumental in this development, even paying for the bridge himself. Other civic improvements in the nineteenth century included the Shire Hall and Cornmarket, both designed by William Owen, the prison by the castle, the workhouse on Priory Mount and the Infirmary on St. Thomas' Green. Many of the impressive non-conformist chapels were also built at this time. As the photographs reveal, new, wide thoroughfares were to be the setting for many parades and celebrations.

The arrival of the railway in 1853 brought about a rapid reduction in sea trade, contributing to the decline of the quayside area, although businesses such as the churnmakers Llewellin's benefited from improved access to wider markets. The town continued to be a centre for the farming community and remained the county town of Pembrokeshire until local government re-organisation in the early 1970s. It has been an important shopping centre for the area for a long time. From the 1860s Commerce House in Market Street was one of Wales' largest department stores, while Ocky White's department store is one of many later successful businesses. Today, as elsewhere, large supermarkets have been established.

More life is now returning to the riverside. Road improvements and a new shopping development are attracting visitors to the town, which is also growing as a centre for touring West Wales. Some of the town's interesting old buildings have been demolished but it is hoped that these photographs will help to preserve the heritage of this centuries-old community.

Golygfeydd o'r Strydoedd
Street Scenes

Maes Pictwn gyda milwyr y Rhyfel Byd Cyntaf yn gorymdeithio heibio i Neuadd y Seiri Rhyddion a Thŷ Chalfont.
Picton Place with First World War troops parading past the Masonic Hall and Chalfont House.

Sgwâr Salutation, a'r odynau calch yng Ngerddi'r Jiwbili, tua 1900.
Salutation Square, showing the lime kilns in Jubilee Gardens, *c*1900.

Moch a bechgyn ysgol ger y cafn yfed yn Sgwâr Salutation, tua 1900.
Pigs and schoolboys at the drinking trough in Salutation Square, *c*1900.

Sgwâr Salutation, 1960au. Mae'r gofeb hon wedi'i chodi yn lle'r cafn yfed.
Salutation Square, 1960s. The memorial has replaced the drinking trough.

Heddlu yn gorymdeithio ym Maes Victoria, tua 1900. Ar draws y Bont Newydd gwelir Warws Gelfi Lewis, a drowyd yn ddiweddarach yn Theatr y Sir.
Marching police in Victoria Place, *c*1900. Across the New Bridge is Lewis's Furniture Warehouse, replaced later by the County Theatre.

CASTLE SQUARE, HAVERFORDWEST.

Sgwâr y Castell yn gynnar yn y ganrif hon.
Castle Square early this century.

Llun gynnar iawn o'r dref o ben uchaf y Stryd Fawr, yn yr 1860au mae'n debyg.
A very early picture of the town from the top of High Street, probably 1860s.

Y Stryd Fawr yn 1907.
High Street in 1907.

Tyrfaoedd yn y Stryd Fawr, tua 1912.
Crowds in High Street, c1912.

Y tu allan i Neuadd y Sir a gyferbyn â'r 'County Club', tua 1900.
Outside the Shire Hall and opposite the County Club, c1900.

Y Stryd Fawr yn yr 1960au.
High Street in the 1960s.

Ceir yn y Stryd Fawr, tua 1928.
Cars in High Street, c1928.

Y Stryd Fawr, gyda Neuadd y Sir wedi'i haddurno, tua 1900.
High Street with the Shire Hall festooned, c1900.

Gang dymchwel wrth eu gwaith yn yr hen Swyddfa Bost, y Stryd Fawr, tua 1900.
A demolition gang at work in the old Post Office, High Street, c1900.

Edrych i lawr Stryd y Farchnad yn yr 1950au gyda siop nwyddau haearn Herbert's ar y dde.
Looking down Market Street in the 1950s with Herbert's ironmonger's shop on the right.

Stryd y Farchnad tua 1910 gyda Commerce House ar y chwith, gyda'r cysgod.
Market Street c1910 with Commerce House on the left, with canopy.

Y baneri yn cyhwfan yn Stryd ar Afr, tua 1900.
Flags out in Goat Street, *c*1900.

Stryd y Rhiw gyda Choleg Tŷ'r Rhiw ar y chwith, tua 1900.
Hill Street with Hill House College on left, c1900.

Lôn Rhosmari wrth agosáu at Goleg Tŷ'r Rhiw.
Rosemary Lane approaching Hill House College.

Pen uchaf Stryd Dewi cyn cyflwyno'r system un-ffordd.
Top of Dew Street, before the one-way system came in.

Pont Myrddin, gyda Thafarn 'Prince of Wales' ar y dde, ar waelod Rhiw Myrddin, tua 1900.
Merlins Bridge, showing, on the right, the Prince of Wales at the bottom of Merlins Hill, *c*1900.

Sgwâr y Morwr, ar gyffordd y Stryd Dywyll a Rhiw'r Tŵr, tua 1910.
Mariner's Square, junction of Dark Street and Tower Hill, c1910.

Gerddi'r Ffynnon, tua 1970. Ym mhen blaen y llun, ar y chwith, mae'r tir lle arferai'r Theatr Fach sefyll.
Spring Gardens, c1970. In the foreground is land on which stood the Little Theatre.

Stryd y Sgubor, tua 1910, gydag, ar y chwith, Elusendai Ymddiriedolaeth Perrot.
Barn Street, *c*1910, showing, on the left, the Perrot Trust Almshouses.

'Klondyke', sef Peter O'Dwyer, un o nifer o 'gymeriadau lliwgar' oedd yn y dref a'r cyffiniau yn yr 1950au.
'Klondyke', Peter O'Dwyer, one of a number of 'characters' about the town in the 1950s.

Stryd y Cei, ar y dde mae hen gelloedd Neuadd y Sir, tua 1910.
Quay Street, on the right the old Shire Hall cells, c1910.

Stryd y Cei, y tu cefn i'r 'Bristol Trader', tua 1900 mae'n debyg.
Quay Street, behind the Bristol Trader, probably c1900.

Stryd y Bont ger y fynedfa i Lôn Tŷ'r Brodyr, gyda Gwesty'r 'Swan' yn y cefndir, tua 1900.
Bridge Street at the entrance to Friars Lane, in the distance the Swan Hotel, *c*1900.

Stryd y Bont, 1930au.
Bridge Street, 1930s.

Ceffylau gwedd ar eu gorau y tu allan i'r 'Farmer's Arms', Holloway, tua 1900.
Showing off the shires outside the Farmer's Arms, Holloway, c1900.

Cartlett, gan edrych draw tuag at y 'Carmarthen Arms', 1960au. Mae'r adeiladau ar y dde wedi'u bwrw lawr bellach.

Cartlett, looking towards town from the Carmarthen Arms, 1960s. The buildings on the right have now gone.

Gerddi'r Jiwbili a Heol Cartlett, 1970au. Gellir gweld olion yr odynau calch ar y dde o hyd.
Jubilee Gardens and Cartlett Road, 1970s. Remnants of the lime kilns can still be seen on the right.

Scotch Corner, gan edrych draw tuag at Scotchwell, 1970au.
Scotch Corner, looking towards Scotchwell, 1970s.

Sgwâr Pen-y-bont, tua 1960, cyn newid y ffordd.
Bridgend Square, c1960, before the new road scheme.

Sgwâr Pen-y-bont gyda Chwmni Gwneud Coetsys Bland ar waelod Prendergast, tua 1900.
Bridgend Square with Bland's Coach Builders at the bottom of Prendergast, c1900.

Y heol i'r dref o 'Bentref' Prendergast, tua 1910.
The road to town from Prendergast 'Village', *c*1910.

Prendergast, tua 1910.
Prendergast, c1910.

Tafarn y 'Bull', Prendergast. W.D. Phillips, yr awdur yw'r un â'r ymbarel, 1930au.
Bull Inn, Prendergast. W.D. Phillips, author with umbrella, 1930s.

Angladd y Dirprwy Brif Gwnstabl Alfred Thomas, 1925. Yr osgordd yn agosáu at Fynwent Stryd Albert ar hyd Stryd y Sgubor.
Funeral of Deputy Chief Constable Alfred Thomas, 1925. Cortège approaching Albert Street Cemetery up Barn Street.

Cornel Stryd y Farchnad a'r Stryd Fawr. Dymchwelwyd yr adeiladau hyn uwch yr hen ddaeargell yn 1952.
Corner of Market Street and High Street. These buildings above the old crypt were demolished in 1952.

Daeargell yn nhŷ masnachwr o'r canol oesoedd, o dan siop ar gornel Stryd y Farchnad a'r Stryd Fawr, 1940au.

Vaulted basement to medieval merchant's house, below shop at corner of Market Street and High Street, 1940s.

Pen uchaf y Stryd Fawr gan edrych tuag at yr Ysgol Ramadeg, tua 1950.
Top of High Street looking towards Grammar School, *c*1950.

YR AIL RAN • SECTION TWO

Glan yr Afon
The Riverside

Golygfa o Hwlffordd o'r Ffrolic, yn dangos Eglwys Tomos Sant a'r castell tua 1900.
A view of Haverfordwest from The Frolic, showing St. Thomas' Church and the castle, *c*1900.

Y bont godi yn Hwlffordd wedi'i gostwng i drenau fynd drosti, tua 1895. Ar y dde gwelir y cwch glo Viola of Chester *yn dadlwytho.*
The railway swing bridge at Haverfordwest in the lowered position, c1895. On the right is the collier *Viola of Chester* unloading.

Y bont rheilffordd yn Hwlffordd wedi'i chodi i ganiatau'r agerlong Cleddau *i fynd heibio, tua 1905.*
The railway swing bridge at Haverfordwest open to allow the passage of SS *Cleddau*, c1905.

Y cwch hwylio Mary Jane Lewis o *Aberdaugleddau ar y cei yn Hwlffordd, tua 1930.*
The sailing boat *Mary Jane Lewis* of Milford on the quayside at Haverfordwest, *c*1930.

Ia ar y Cleddau Wen ger yr Hen Bont, hefyd gwelir siop Thomas y Cigydd, 1960au.
Ice on the Western Cleddau at Old Bridge, also showing the shop of Thomas the Butcher, 1960s.

Cwch glo a chwlm wedi angori wrth y cei gerllaw'r iard lo y tu ôl i Ystordy Archie Griffiths ger Stryd yr Hen Bont, tua 1900. Mae'r fan hon yn rhan o Ganolfan Siopa Cei Glan yr afon erbyn hyn.
A coal and culm barge moored at the quay alongside the coal yard behind Archie Griffiths' Warehouse, off Old Bridge Street, c1900. This is now part of Riverside Quay Shopping Centre.

Golygfa ar hyd y Cei Newydd o'r Rhodfa gyda chwch glo yn dadlwytho, tua 1900.
A view along the New Quay from the Parade with a collier unloading, *c*1900.

Y rhan uchaf o'r cei islaw yr Hen Bont tua 1900. Gwelir yma y morfa a adenillwyd yn ddiweddarach. Mae Canolfan Siopa Cei Glan yr afon ar y safle hwn yn awr.
The upper quay area below Old Bridge, *c*1900. This shows the saltings which were later reclaimed. Riverside Quay Shopping Centre is now on the site.

Y Bont Newydd o'r hen faes parcio, 1960au, lle mae Canolfan Siopa Cei Glan yr afon wedi'i lleoli yn awr. Mae hen Theatr y Sir i'w gweld y tu ôl i'r bont.
New Bridge from the old car park, where Riverside Quay Shopping Centre is now situated, 1960s. The former County Theatre can be seen behind the bridge.

Y Gors yn nhu blaen y llun a'r Hen Gei, tua 1900. Yn y canol, yn y tu blaen, mae tafarn y 'Bristol Trader' a Thŷ Hermons Hill i'r dde ar ochr y bryn. Mae nifer o'r ystordai wedi diflannu erbyn hyn.

The Marsh in the foreground and Old Quay, c1900. In the centre foreground is the Bristol Trader inn, with Hermons Hill House to the right on the hillside. Several warehouses have since disappeared.

Y Castell a Ffowndri'r Cleddau, tua 1890, o ochr arall y morfa ar y lan ddwyreiniol.
Castle and the Cleddau Foundry, *c*1890, from across the saltings on the east bank.

Y gored islaw'r Bont Newydd, gyda Theatr y Sir ar y dde.
The weir below New Bridge, with the County Theatre on the right.

Achlysuron Arbennig
Special Events

Y seremoni swyddogol i ddadorchuddio Cofeb y Rhyfel Byd Cyntaf, ar Fedi'r 3ydd, 1921. Dangosir y Gofeb yn ei safle gwreiddiol yn Sgwâr Salutation, gerllaw'r fynedfa i Scotchwell.

The official ceremony of the unveiling of the First World War Memorial, 3 September 1921. The Memorial is shown in its original position in Salutation Square, adjacent to the entrance to Scotchwell.

Dengys y llun y Gofeb yn cael ei symud i'w safle presennol gerllaw Neuadd y Seiri Rhyddion.

The photograph shows a stage in the moving of the War Memorial to its present position at the side of the Masonic Hall.

Aelodau o Urdd Frenhinol Hynafol y 'Buffalo' yn gorymdeithio drwy Sgwâr y Morwr i fynd i wasanaeth coffa'r Brenin Edward VII.

Members of the Royal Antediluvian Order of Buffaloes parading through Mariner's Square to attend the memorial service to King Edward VII.

Gorymdaith gan aelodau o gymdeithas gyfeillgar leol drwy Stryd y Farchnad, Hwlffordd, tua 1920.

A procession down Market Street, Haverfordwest, involving members of a local friendly society, *c*1920.

Milwyr ar barêd y tu allan i'r hen Neuadd Ddril yng Ngerddi'r Jiwbili, Hwlffordd, yn ystod y Rhyfel Byd Cyntaf.
Troops parading outside the former Drill Hall in Jubilee Gardens, Haverfordwest, during the First World War.

David Lloyd George yn annerch torf yn Hwlffordd, Tachwedd 1922.
David Lloyd George giving a speech to an attentive crowd in Haverfordwest, November 1922.

*Aelod Seneddol newydd Sir Benfro yn cael ei gludo ar gadair uwchben y dorf i mewn i
Sgwâr y Morwr ar ôl Is-etholiad 1908.*
After the by-election of 1908 the new member for Pembrokeshire is shown being chaired
into Mariner's Square.

Torf fawr wedi ymgynnull o flaen Neuadd y Sir yn ystod etholiad 1910.
A large crowd gathered in front of the Shire Hall during the 1910 election.

Dadorchuddio Cofeb Rhyfel De Affrica ger Eglwys y Santes Fair, Hydref 21ain, 1904 gyda band yr heddlu yn chwarar.
The unveiling of the South African War Memorial by St. Mary's Church, 21 October 1904, with a police band playing.

Tai yn Nheras Caerloyw, Hwlffordd, wedi'u haddurno, fe gredir i ddathlu codi'r gwarchae ar Mafeking, Mai 1900.

Houses in Gloucester Terrace, Haverfordwest, believed to be decorated to celebrate the Relief of Mafeking, May 1900.

Milwyr oedd wedi dychwelyd o Ryfel y Boeriaid yn gorymdeithio heibio i Neuadd y Seiri Rhyddion.

Troops returning from the Boer War marching past the Masonic Hall.

Plant ysgol Sul wedi ymgynnull yn Sgwâr y Castell i wrando ar anerchiad adeg coroni'r Brenin Sior V, 1911.
Sunday school children assembled in Castle Square listening to a speech on the occasion of the coronation of King George V, 1911.

Plant wedi ymgynnull i gael parti i ddathlu Jiwbili Arian Brenin Sior V, yn Neuadd y Farchnad, Stryd y Farchnad, ar Fai'r 7fed, 1935.
Children gather for a party to celebrate King George V's Silver Jubilee, at the Market Hall, Market Street, 7 May 1935.

Y Frenhines Elizabeth II yn cael ei chroesawu gan dyrfaoedd mawr ger Neuadd y Seiri Rhyddion wrth ymweld â'r dref yn 1967.

Her Majesty Queen Elizabeth II being greeted by large crowds near the Masonic Hall on her visit to the town in 1967.

John Evans, Uchel Siryf Sir Benfro, gydag uchel swyddogion eraill ac aelodau o'r heddlu lleol y tu allan i Westy'r Castell, tua 1900.

John Evans, High Sheriff of Pembrokeshire, with other dignitaries and members of the local constabulary outside the Castle Hotel, c1900.

Torf lawen yn croesawu Maer Prendergast, tua 1900.
A cheerful crowd of onlookers greeting the Mayor of Prendergast, *c*1900.

Golygfa yn un o strydoedd Prendergast yn ystod y dathliadau adeg sefydlu'r maer newydd, tua 1900.
A street scene in Prendergast during the celebrations for their new mayor, *c*1900.

Mrs Massey, o'r Swffragetiaid, yn annerch torf yn Sgwâr y Castell, tua 1910.
Mrs Massey of the Suffragettes speaking to a crowd in Castle Square, *c*1910.

Y Cadfridog Booth, o Fyddin yr Iachawdwriaeth, mewn car agored y tu allan i Erddi'r Ffynnon, Hwlffordd, tua 1910.
General Booth of the Salvation Army is seen here in an open-topped car outside Spring Gardens, Haverfordwest, c1910.

Agor Scotchwell, tua 1908.
This photograph shows the opening of Scotchwell, *c*1908.

Masnach
Commerce

Y Ffair Wartheg ar borfa Maes Tomos Sant tua 1900. Mae'r rhes tai a welir yn cynnwys Siop Hen Bethau Gerald Oliver heddiw.

The Cattle Fair on a grassy St. Thomas' Green, c1900. The row of houses today includes Gerald Oliver's Antique Shop.

Defaid ar werth ym Mryn Myrddin tua 1900. Mae'n amlwg bod digon o oleuadau nwy yn y stryd.

Sheep for sale, Merlins Hill, *c*1900. The street was clearly well supplied with gas lights.

Marchnad wartheg ar lan yr afon yn Hwlffordd ym mhumdegau'r ganrif hon. Y tu draw, yn y canol, gwelir Gwaith Buddeiau Llewellin ac i'r chwith mae Eglwys Bresbyteraidd Ebeneser.

Haverfordwest riverside cattle market, 1950s. Beyond are, in the centre, Llewellin's Churnworks and, left of centre, Ebenezer Presbyterian Church.

John Lewellin a gweithwyr Gwaith Buddeiau Llewellin, tua 1890. Roedd John Llewellin y drydedd genhedlaeth o'r teulu i weithio yn y busnes. Bu'n llwyddiannus iawn yn dyfeisio peiriannau newydd, fel y Fuddai Dro Echreiddig, a'u gwerthu ledled y byd. Roedd y gweithwyr yn grefftus iawn a'u cyflog, o'r herwydd, yn dda. Yn ôl ymwelydd dienw yn 1896, 'nid oedd sôn am waith gwael yn unman yn yr adeilad.'

John Llewellin and the workforce at Llewellin's Churnworks, c1890. John Llewellin represented the third generation in the business. He was very successful, introducing new products like the Eccentric End-Over Churn and marketing them all over the world. The workers were very skilled and their wages correspondingly good. An anonymous visitor in 1896 reported that 'scamped work is unknown within the premises.'

Gwneud profion, yn 1929, ar beiriant cymysgu menyn mawr a gynhyrchwyd gan Llewellin. Gwelir Mr A. J. Birt Llewellin (mewn côt wen), un o gyfarwyddwyr yr hen gwmni teuluol hwn, yn goruchwylio'r profion. Ar y chwith gwelir buddai fenyn a chymysgwr wedi'u cyfuno ar gyfer gwaith mewn ffatri.

Testing a large Llewellin butter-blending machine in 1929. Mr A.J. Birt Llewellin (in white coat), a director of the long-established family firm, supervises. On the left is a combined factory butter churn and blender.

Gwaith Buddeiau Llewellin ym Mhorth y Gogledd yn ystod yr adeg yr oedd yn cael ei ddymchwel i wneud lle ar gyfer y gylchfan newydd. Mae modurdy Bland yn sefyll ar ran o'r safle heddiw. Ar ddechrau'r ganrif y Gwaith Buddeiau oedd y cyflogwr mwyaf yn y dref.

Llewellin's Churnworks at North Gate during demolition in 1987 to make way for a new roundabout. Bland's garage now stands on part of the site. The churnworks was the town's largest employer early this century.

Melin bapur osgeiddig Prendergast, a adeiladwyd o friciau, ar draws ffos oedd yn dwyn dwr o'r Cleddau Wen rhwng Cottesmore a Glanafon, tua 1900. Malu ŷd oedd y felin yn wreiddiol ond fe'i hail-adeiladwyd yn y 1760au fel melin gotwm ond cynhyrchu papur y bu yn ystod y rhan fwyaf o'r bedwaredd ganrif ar bymtheg.

The elegant brick Prendergast paper mill, *c*1900, located on a leet off the Western Cleddau between Cottesmore and Glanafon. Originally a corn mill, it was rebuilt in the 1760s as a cotton mill but was producing paper for most of the nineteenth century.

Iard Goed a Melin Lifio Cartlett ar ochr ddwyreiniol y Cleddau rhwng Picton Place a Cambrian Place, tua diwedd y bedwaredd ganrif ar bymtheg.

Cartlett Sawmill and Timberyard on the east bank of the Cleddau between Picton Place and Cambrian Place, late nineteenth century.

Gweithwyr yn aros i dynnu eu llun yn ystod y gwaith o adeiladu'r Woolworths gwreiddiol yn Heol y Bont yn 1929.

Workmen pose for the camera during preparations for the building of the town's original Woolworths in Bridge Street in 1929.

Gwesty'r Castell, tua 1910. Fe'i dymchwelwyd yn rhannol yn ddiweddarach. Sylwch ar y modur a'r goets o flaen y fynedfa.
Castle Hotel, c1910. It was later partially demolished. Note both carriage and motor car at front entrance.

Ffermwyr yn gwrthdystio yn erbyn prisiau amaethyddol yn Sgwâr y Castell, 1960au.
Farmers demonstrate against agricultural prices in Castle Square, 1960s.

Golygfa brin o gysylltfur de Castell Hwlffordd o Sgwâr y Castell yn y 1950au cyn i Woolworths gael ei adeiladu.

A rare view of the south curtain wall of Haverfordwest Castle from Castle Square in the 1950s before the construction of Woolworths.

Tudalen canlynol: gwesty'r 'Swan', Sgwâr y Swan, tua 1970. Roedd yr adeilad a ddymchwelwyd yn fuan ar ôl tynnu'r llun, yn dyddio'n ôl i 1536. Daeth archfarchnad ar y safle ar ôl hyn, ac wedyn daeth Rayers.

Following page: the Swan Hotel, Swan Square, c1970. The building, parts of which dated back to 1536, was demolished shortly afterwards and replaced by a supermarket which later became Rayers.

Isaiah Reynolds, gwerthwr bwyd, menyn, hadau a gwrtaith, Sgwâr y Swan, Hwlffordd, tua 1910. Mae'r ceffyl a'r cert yn sefyll ym mhen isaf Holloway.

Isaiah Reynolds, provision dealer, butter, seed and manure merchant, Swan Square, Haverfordwest, *c*1910. The horse and cart is standing at the bottom of Holloway.

Siop ddillad gyffredinol S.G. Phillips, Sgwâr y Castell, 1920au.
S.G. Phillips' general drapers shop, Castle Square, 1920s.

Siop gynharach Hadfield yn 23–25 Stryd y Bont, tua 1910. Symudodd y siop, oedd yn arbenigo mewn fframiau lluniau a nwyddau ffansi, i 29 Y Stryd Fawr yn fuan ar ôl hyn.
Hadfield's earlier shop at 23–25 Bridge Street, probably c1910. The shop, specialising in picture frames and fancy goods, moved to 29 High Street soon afterwards.

Hadfield's Bazaar, 29 Y Stryd Fawr, yn y 1920au. Yn sefyll wrth ddrws y siop hon, oedd yn gwerthu teganau a nwyddau ffansi, gwelir Emma Hadfield â'i mab, William â'i hwyres, Mabel.

Hadfield's Bazaar, 29 High Street, in the 1920s. Standing in the doorway of this toy and fancy goods shop are Emma Hadfield with her son, William, and grand daughter, Mabel.

Siop nwyddau haearn, cyllyll a nwyddau plymwr, Stephen Green, yn y Stryd Fawr, rhwng Bisley Munt a Neuadd y Sir, tua 1910. Mae'n debyg bod y beiciau ar werth.
Stephen Green's ironmongers, cutlers and plumbers shop, High Street, between Bisley Munt and the Shire Hall, *c*1910. Presumably the bicycles were for sale.

Siop gyntaf Ocky White yn y Stryd Fawr. Symudodd y busnes i Heol y Bont yn 1929.
The first Ocky White shop in High Street. The business was moved to Bridge Street in 1929.

Siop deiliwr a siop ddillad Beers yn Stryd yr Hen Bont tua 1910. Mae'r ffenestri arbennig wedi hen ddiflannu ond mae'r siop yn bod o hyd fel County Sports.
Beers drapers and tailors shop, Old Bridge Street, c1910. The elaborate window frames have been replaced but the shop still exists as County Sports.

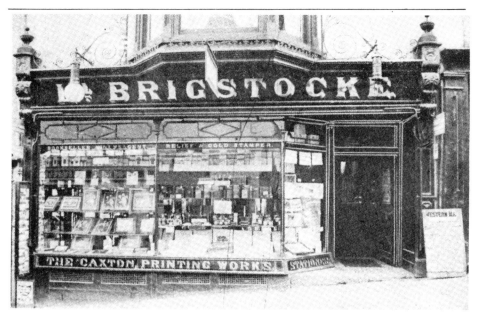

Brigstocke, argraffwr a gwerthwr llyfrau, papurau newydd, papur ysgrifennu a nwyddau ffansi, 18 Stryd y Farchnad, tua 1910. Dyma siop y West Wales Guardian heddiw.
Brigstocke's, printer, bookseller, stationer, newsagent and fancy goods dealer, 18 Market Street, c1910. Today this is the West Wales Guardian shop.

J. a J.P. Reynolds, siop groser a masnachwyr, 33 Y Stryd Fawr, tua 1910. Roeddent yn hawlio 'Nid oes cig moch gwell i'w gael yn unman.'
J. & J.P. Reynolds, family grocers and provision merchants, 33 High Street, c1910. They claimed: 'Our smoked breakfast bacon is unsurpassed.'

Canolfan Dybaco Hwlffordd, y Stryd Fawr, yn yr 1930au mae'n debyg.
The Haverfordwest Tobacco Centre, High Street, probably 1930s.

Yr hen Neudd Farchnad yn Stryd y Farchnad a adeiladwyd yn 1827. Cynlluniwyd yr adeilad cymesur hwn gan bensaer hynotaf y dref yn y bedwaredd ganrif a'r bymtheg, sef William Owen. Nid o'r farchnad hon y daw'r enw Stryd y Farchnad ond o farchnad a gynhaliwyd o gwmpas Eglwys y Santes Fair yn y canol oesoedd.

The old Market Hall in Market Street, built in 1827. This finely proportioned building was designed by the town's most prominent nineteenth-century architect, William Owen. The name Market Street derives not from this market but from the medieval market which was held around St. Mary's Church.

Ail-luniwyd ffasâd y Farchnad yn 1933 a dyma sut yr edrychai yn 1949. Ar ochr isaf y llun gwelir arwydd ysblennydd yn hysbysebu 'The Elite Salon, Ladies' Hairdressers'.

The 1933 replacement façade to the Market Hall photographed in 1949. On the downhill side is an elaborate painted sign for 'The Elite Salon, Ladies' Hairdressers'.

Y BUMED RAN • SECTION FIVE

Trafnidiaeth
Transport

Tollborth rhwng y Bont Newydd a Maes Victoria, ddiwedd y bedwaredd ganrif ar bymtheg. Mae dwy lamp nwy wedi'u cynnwys fel rhan o'r rhwystr.
Tollgate between New Bridge and Victoria Place, late nineteenth century. Two gas lights have been incorporated into the barrier.

Yr orsaf reilffordd o Cartlett gyda'r 'Masons Arms' ar y chwith a'r 'Queen's Hotel' ar y dde, tua 1900.
The railway station from Cartlett with the Masons Arms on the left and the Queen's Hotel on the right, c1900.

Edrych tuag at ganol y dref o fan gerllaw yr orsaf reilffordd, tua 1900 mae'n debyg. Gwesty oedd yr adeilad sydd ychydig i'r chwith o'r canol.
Looking towards the town centre from just outside the railway station, probably c1900. The building left of centre was a hotel.

Trên ager yn croesi'r bont godi dros Afon Cleddau, tua 1890. Rheolwyd y bont gan y caban arwyddion ar y dde.

A steam train crossing the lifting bridge over the Cleddau, *c*1890. The bridge was controlled from the signal box on the right.

Yr orsaf reilffordd brysur gyda lle croesi dan do dros y traciau, tua 1910 mae'n debyg.
The busy railway station with covered walkway over the tracks, probably *c*1910.

Tractor ager yn tynnu dau ôl-gerbyd o gyfeiriad y Bont Newydd i Faes Victoria, tua 1900.
A traction engine pulling two trailers from the New Bridge into Victoria Place, *c*1900.

*Gosod concrid yn Heol Cartlett, tua 1930. Mae Garej Green ar y chwith, mae Garej Bland
yn yr cefndir, a'r hen odynau calch a siop teiliwr Voyle ar y dde.*
Concrete laying in Cartlett Road, c1930. Green's Garage is on the left, Bland's Garage is in
the background, and the old lime kilns and Voyle's tailors shop are on the right.

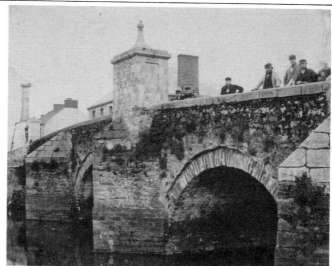

Yr Hen Bont o'r gogledd, ddiwedd y bedwaredd ganrif ar bymtheg. Ail-godwyd y bont hon yn 1726. Syr John Philipps o Bictwn a dalodd am y gwaith. Mae nifer o bobl wedi oedi ar y bont i wylio'r ffotograffydd wrth ei waith.

The Old Bridge from the north, late nineteenth century. This bridge was rebuilt in 1726 and paid for by Sir John Philipps of Picton. There seems to have been a lot of interest in the photographer from bystanders on the bridge.

Damwain ar waelod Rhiw Prendergast. Mae'n ymddangos bod wagen ffair neu syrcas wedi moelyd, 1905.

An accident involving what appears to be an overturned fairground or circus wagon near the bottom of Prendergast Hill, 1905.

Eric Green y gyrru car Ford lan y stepiau ym mhen uchaf y Stryd Fawr yn 1912. Stynt i gael cyhoeddusrwydd oedd hyn.
Eric Green driving a Ford car up steps at the top of High Street in 1912. This was a publicity stunt.

Mr Holt yn gyrru un o geir cyntaf Green's Motors, y tu allan i gatiau Scotchwell, tua 1910.
Mr Holt driving one of Green's first motor cars outside Scotchwell Gates, *c*1910.

Garej Green's yn Heol Cartlett, tua 1910. Daeth stiop 'Kwik Save' yno yn ddiweddarach.
Dymchwelwyd yr adeilad yn yr 1980au i wneud lle i faes parcio aml-lawr. Ar y pryd gallai
Green's ymffrostio taw dyma'r 'garej fwyaf a'r orau yn yr ardal'.
Green's Garage in Cartlett Road, *c*1910. The building later became Kwik Save and was
demolished in the 1980s to make way for a multi-storey car park. At the time, Green's
boasted that it was 'the largest and best equipped garage in the district'.

Un o fysiau 'Green's Motors' y tu allan i'r Garej, tua 1910.
A Green's Motors bus outside Green's Garage, c1910.

Un o fysiau 'Green's Motors', gyda bysiau eraill y tu cefn, a'r staff yn sefyll o flaen y bws, tua 1930.
A Green's Motors bus, with others behind and staff in front, c1930.

Sefydliadau
Institutions

Gwasanaeth Boreol yn Ysgol Uwchradd Fodern Hwlffordd, 1950au.
Assembly at Haverfordwest Secondary Modern School, 1950s.

Ysgol Ramadeg Hwlffordd, Stryd Dewi, tua 1920.
Haverfordwest Grammar School, Dew Street, c1920.

Ysgol Mary Tasker, Rhiw'r Tŵr, tua 1900.
Mary Tasker's School, Tower Hill, c1900.

Ysgol Ramadeg y Bechgyn, Hwlffordd, tua 1913.
Haverfordwest Grammar School boys, *c*1913.

Miss A. Barwell, prif athrawes gyntaf Ysgol Tasker, 1892.
Miss A. Barwell, first headmistress of Tasker's School, 1892.

Y disgybl cyntaf yn Ysgol Tasker, Marie Louise Davies; fe'i ganed yn 1877. Tynnwyd y llun yn 1896.
The first pupil of Tasker's School, Marie Louise Davies, born 1877. Photograph taken 1896.

Merched o Ysgol Tasker, 1912.
Girls from Tasker's School, 1912.

Disgyblion y tu allan i Dŷ Kensington, Ysgol Tasker, 1950au.
Pupils outside Kensington House, Tasker's School, 1950s.

Cwmni Drama Ysgol Tasker, Rhagfyr 1927. Y ddrama oedd Uncle Remus.
Tasker's School dramatics, December 1927. The play was *Uncle Remus*.

Dawnsio o amgylch y fedwen Fai, Ysgol Stryd y Sgubor, diwedd y bedwaredd ganrif ar bymtheg.
Maypole dancing, Barn Street V.C. School, late nineteenth century.

Coleg Tŷ'r Rhiw, Stryd y Rhiw, tua 1905.
Hill House College, Hill Street, *c*1905.

Y chwiorydd Davies, Agnes ac Emily, merched y Dr Thomas Davies, gyferbyn, a redai Coleg Tŷ'r Rhiw. Mae'n debyg y tynnwyd y llun hwn yn yr 1920au.
Hill House College was run by the two Davies sisters, Agnes and Emily, who were the daughters of Dr Thomas Davies, opposite. Probably taken in the 1920s.

Y Parchedig Ddoctor Thomas Davies, Prifathro Coleg y Bedyddwyr, Stryd y Rhiw, o 1856 tan 1894. Byddai'r llun hwn wedi'i dynnu yn ystod ei flynyddoedd cynharaf yn y swydd. Roedd yn Weinidog hefyd ar Eglwys Bethesda, gyda'r Bedyddwyr.

The Reverend Doctor Thomas Davies, Principal of the Baptist College, Hill Street, from 1856 until 1894. This photograph would have been taken during his early years in the post. He was also the Pastor of Bethesda Baptist Church.

Ysgol Prendergast o'r Gelli Geirios, tua 1914.
Prendergast School from Cherry Grove, *c*1914.

Ystafell ddosbarth yn Ysgol Prendergast, tua 1914.
A classroom in Prendergast School, *c*1914.

Dosbarth yn Ysgol y Merched, Prendergast, 1916.
A class at Prendergast Girls' School, 1916.

Plant bach yn dawnsio yn Ysgol Prendergast, 1920au.
Infants dancing at Prendergast School, 1920s.

Dosbarth y plant bach, Ysgol Prendergast, 1920au.
Classroom for infants, Prendergast School, 1920s.

Lleiniau i dyfu cnydau y tu cefn i Ysbyty Tomos Sant, Lôn y Wins, yn gynnar yn yr ugeinfed ganrif.

Cultivation strips behind St. Thomas' Hospital, Winch Lane, early twentieth century.

Llun a dynnwyd yn 1937 o adfail adeilad canoloesol ym Mhont Myrddin – credai pobl yr ardal taw tŷ i'r gwahanglwyfion ydoedd 'slawer dydd.

The remains, in 1937, of a medieval building at Merlins Bridge, reputedly a leper house.

Coridor o gelloedd yng Ngharchar Hwlffordd, a godwyd yn 1820 o fewn muriau allanol y castell.

A corridor of cells in Haverfordwest Prison, built in 1820 within the outer ward of the castle.

Cyferbyn: diwrnod agoriadol Amgueddfa a Swyddfa Archifau Sir Benfro ar Ebrill 11eg, 1967. Gwelir Robert Kennedy, y curadur oedd newydd ei benodi, canol y llun, yn dangos cyllell clocsiwr i Syr Ben Bowen Thomas, ar y dde. Cafodd yr hen garchar, a godwyd yn 1820, ei addasu i fod yn gartref i'r Amgueddfa a'r Swyddfa Archifau.

Opposite: on the opening day of the Pembrokeshire County Museum and Record Office on 11 April 1967, Robert Kennedy, the freshly appointed curator, centre, demonstrates a clogger's knife to Sir Ben Bowen Thomas, right. The building was converted from the 1820 prison.

Y carchar ar dir y castell, yn yr 1950au mae'n debyg. Mae'r tŵr a'r rhesaid o adeiladau ar y dde wedi'u dymchwel.
The prison at the castle, probably in the 1950s. Both the tower and the range on the right have been demolished.

Nyrsys yn yr Ysbyty, Maes Tomos Sant, 1894. Rhes flaen, o'r chwith i'r dde: C. Lloyd, M. Owens, Miss Ball (Metron), N. Machin, S.P. Spratt. Rhes gefn, o'r chwith i'r dde: M. Russell, L Tranter, M. Goring, S. Rawlinson.

Nurses at the Infirmary, St. Thomas' Green, 1894. Front, left to right: C. Lloyd, M. Owens, Miss Ball (Matron), N. Machin, S.P. Spratt. Back, left to right: M. Russell, L. Tranter, M. Goring, S. Rawlinson.

Yr Ysbyty, Maes Tomos, tua 1910.
The Infirmary, St. Thomas' Green, *c*1910.

Ysbyty Coffa y Sir, Lôn y Wins, 1930au. Dymchwelwyd yr adeiladau, ar ôl mynd rhwng y cŵn a'r brain am flynyddoedd, yn gynnar yn yr 1990au.
The County War Memorial Hospital, Winch Lane, 1930s. The buildings were demolished, after years of dereliction, in the early 1990s.

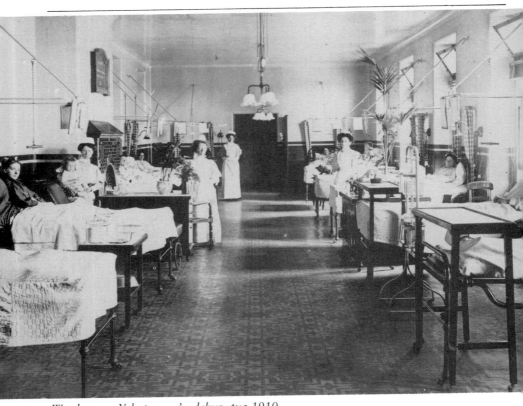

Ward, yn yr Ysbyty mae'n debyg, tua 1910.
A ward, probably in the Infirmary, c1910.

Hen Ysbyty Llwynhelyg, tua 1970.
The old Withybush Hospital, *c*1970.

Y Neuadd Ddril, Gerddi'r Jiwbili, 1980au. Fe'u dymchwelwyd yn ddiweddar.
The Drill Hall, Jubilee Gardens, 1980s. It was recently demolished.

Prif Swyddfa Bost y Dref, ym mhen uchaf y Stryd Fawr yr adeg honno, gyda'r staff wedi ymgynnull y tu allan, tua 1910.
The town's main Post Office, then at the top of High Street, with staff assembled outside, *c*1910.

Codi'r Neuadd Ddirwest, Stryd y Santes Fair, 1880au.
Construction work on the Temperance Hall, St. Mary's Street, 1880s.

Y Frigâd Dân yng ngharnifal yr ysbyty, Gorffennaf 1933. Mae'r hen injan dân o 1892, a dynnid gan geffylau, ar y dde. Yn sefyll yn y rhes flaen, gyda'r Frigâd, y mae, o'r chwith: Pugh Davies, Fferyllydd; Eric Green, Cwmni Moduron Green; Sidney Morgan, Adeiladwr; Owain Thomas, Pensaer; a Mr Garry Fitzgerald.

The Fire Brigade at a hospital carnival, July 1933. The 1892 horse-drawn engine is on the right. Standing in front, with the Brigade, are, from left: Pugh Davies, Chemist; Eric Green, of Green's Motors; Sidney Morgan, Builder; Owain Thomas, Architect; and Mr Garry Fitzgerald.

Adeiladau Crefyddol
Religious Buildings

Adfeilion yr hen briordy, yn drwch o dyfiant, tua 1900 mae'n debyg.
The old priory ruins, much overgrown, probably c1900.

Eglwys Ishel Sant, Haroldston, fel yr oedd yn y bedwaredd ganrif ar bymtheg. Gosodwyd to newydd a ffenestri newydd yn 1894.

Haroldston St. Issell's Church as it looked in the nineteenth century. It was given a new roof and windows in 1894.

Eglwys San Martin cyn ail-godi'r meindwr, 1864–65.

St. Martin's Church before the stone spire was replaced, 1864–65.

Eglwys Tomos Sant o gyfeiriad y de-orllewin, tua 1900.
St. Thomas' Church from the south-west, *c*1900.

Eglwys y Santes Fair, o'r Stryd Fawr. Mae Ysgol Ramadeg y Bechgyn yn y cefndir ar y chwith. Tynnwyd y llun hwn cyn dymchwel siambr y cyngor – yn ymyl tŵr y cloc – yn 1863. Sylwch ar yr hen ffenestr ym mhen blaen yr eglwys a newidiwyd yn 1893.

St. Mary's Church, taken from the High Street. The Boys' Grammar School is in the background on the left. This photograph was taken prior to the demolition of the council chamber – adjoining the clock tower – in 1863. Notice the old window at the front of the church. It was replaced in 1893.

Golwg ar y tu mewn i Eglwys San Martin – llun a dynnwyd yn 1914, ar ddechrau'r Rhyfel Byd Cyntaf.

Interior view of St. Martin's Church taken in the year of the outbreak of the First World War, 1914.

Yr olygfa i lawr Stryd y Sgubor gyda Chapel Bethesda, a godwyd yn 1880, ar y dde. Mae Eglwys San Martin yn y cefndir, tua 1900.

A view down Barn Street with Bethesda Chapel, built 1880, on the right in the foreground. St. Martin's Church is in the background. Taken c1900.

Eglwys Dewi Sant, Prendergast, yn gynnar yn yr ugeinfed ganrif. Ail-godwyd yr eglwys hon yn 1867.

St. David's Church, Prendergast, early twentieth century. This church was rebuilt in 1867.

Rheithordy Prendergast, 1908.

Prendergast Rectory, 1908.

Y Parchedig Owen Jacobs, Eglwys Annibynnol Albany. Ymddeolodd yn 1920 ar ôl gwasanaethu'r Capel am dair blynedd ar hugain.

Reverend Owen Jacobs of Albany Congregational Church. He retired in 1920 after twenty-three years at the church.

Dathliadau 350 mlwyddiant Eglwys Ddiwygiedig Albany yn 1988. Rhes flaen: Mrs Mabel Jones, Mrs a'r Parchedig Emyr Jones, Mrs Gladys Goodridge, Mrs Violet Owen (Organyddes). Rhes gefn: Leslie Thomas, Ray Codd, Mrs Dorothy Lloyd, W.G. Lloyd, G.B. Williams.

Albany Reformed Church 350th Anniversary celebrations in 1988. Front row: Mrs Mabel Jones, Mrs and the Reverend Emyr Jones, Mrs Gladys Goodridge, Mrs Violet Owen (Organist). Back row: Leslie Thomas, Roy Codd, Mrs Dorothy Lloyd, W.G. Lloyd, G.B. Williams.

Eglwys Albany yn 1949. Fe'i hadweinid gynt fel y 'Green Meeting House'. Fe'i sefydlwyd yn 1638.

Albany Congregational Church, formerly the Green Meeting House, in 1949. It was founded in 1638.

Cynulleidfa yn ymgynnull y tu allan i Gapel y Methodistiaid, 1950au.
A congregation gathers outside the Wesleyan Methodist Chapel, 1950s.

Capel y Wesleaid yn Heol Perrot. Nid yw'r rheiliau yno bellach.
The Wesleyan Chapel in Perrot Road. The railings have since been removed.

Capel y Morafiaid ar Faes Tomos Sant, a godwyd yn 1773 ond sydd wedi'i ddymchwel bellach. Tynnwyd y llun ym mis Tachwedd 1959.
The Moravian Chapel on St. Thomas' Green, originally built in 1773 and now demolished. Taken November 1959.

Capel a Neuadd Hill Park, 1957. Agorwyd y Capel Bedyddwyr hwn yn 1856.
Hill Park Baptist Chapel and Hall, 1957. The chapel was opened in 1856.

Grŵp Ysgol Sul Hill Park, 1957.
Hill Park Sunday School group, 1957.

Capel Annibynnol y Tabernacl, ar ôl ei ail-godi yn 1874.
Tabernacle Congregational Chapel after its rebuilding in 1874.

Hamddena
Recreation

Golygfa o'r ffair a gynhaliwyd yng Ngerddi'r Jiwbili, a'r castell yn y cefndir, tua 1900.
Fairground scene, Jubilee Gardens, with castle beyond, *c*1900.

Helter-skelter 'Daddy White', Ffair Portfield, 1920au. Mae Sid White ar y grisiau yn gwisgo het fowler.
Daddy White's Helter-skelter, Portfield Fair, 1920s. Sid White is on the steps, wearing a bowler hat.

Ffair Portfield, tua 1900.
Fairground scene, Portfield Fair, *c*1900.

Gorymdaith y Syrcas ar hyd Heol Cartlett, tua 1900. Mae'r ceirt yn ymestyn yn ôl ar hyd Stryd yr Hen Bont. Mae gwylwyr yn sefyll ar ben yr odyn galch ar y dde.
Circus parade, Cartlett Road, *c*1910. The floats stretch back around the corner along Old Bridge Street. Spectators are crowded on top of the lime kiln on the right.

Rhedwyr ym Maes Victoria, tua 1910.
Long-distance runners in Victoria Place, c1910.

Mae'n ymddangos bod dafad a llew byw yn sefyll yn ddiddig ochr yn ochr ar ben cart syrcas yng ngorymdaith y syrcas drwy Heol Cartlett, tua 1910.
A live lion and sheep are apparently standing contentedly on top of this circus parade float, Cartlett Road, c1910.

Gorymdaith y syrcas drwy Faes Victoria, tua 1910.
A circus parade in Victoria Place, *c*1910.

Gorymdaith y carnifal yn croesi'r Bont Newydd, tua 1910.
Probably a carnival procession passing over New Bridge, c1910.

Carafan draddodiadol un o wŷr y syrcas ar Faes Tomos Sant, tua 1890.
A showman's horse-drawn caravan on St. Thomas' Green, c1890.

Torfeydd yn rhodianna yn Scotchwell ar ddiwrnod o haf i gyfeiliant y band, tua 1910.
Summer crowds at Scotchwell with a band playing, c1910.

Y band yn chwarae yn Scotchwell, tua 1910.
A band playing at Scotchwell, c1910.

Y stondin Bournvita yng nghyntedd Theatr y Sir yn ystod ymgyrch i hyrwyddo ffilm ffars The Happiest Days of Your Life *yn 1950.*
The Bournvita stand in the foyer of the County Theatre during the heavily promoted showing of the post-war farce *The Happiest Days of Your Life* in 1950.

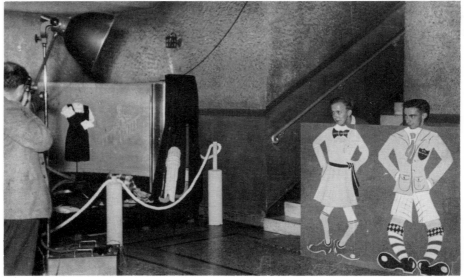

Cael tynnu llun y tu ôl i luniau o ffigurau o'r ffilm The Happiest Days of Your Life *yng nghyntedd y Theatr y Sir, 1950. Enillodd rheolwr y sinema, Mr Shaw, wobr am hyrwyddo'r ffilm sy'n ymwneud â chamgymeriad ar ran y weinyddiaeth gyda'r canlyniad bod ysgol i ferched yn cael ei lleoli ar safle ysgol i fechgyn.*
Posing for photographs behind painted figures from *The Happiest Days of Your Life* in the County Theatre foyer, 1950. The cinema manager, Mr Shaw, won an award for his promotion of the film, the plot of which involves a ministry mistake which billets a girls' school on a boys' school.

Drama ystafell ddosbarth yn Theatr y Sir adeg perfformio The Happiest Days of Your Life, *1950.*
A schoolroom drama at the County Theatre during the run of *The Happiest Days of Your Life*, 1950.

Hysbysebu'r ffilm boblogaidd o'r 1950au The Happiest Days of Your Life, *yn Theatr y Sir.* Promoting the 1950s film *The Happiest Days of Your Life*, then showing at the County Theatre.

Parti gwisg ffansi yn 1922.
A fancy dress party in 1922.

Dawns tenis yn Neuadd y Seiri Rhyddion yn 1923.
A tennis dance at the Masonic Hall in 1923.

Y *'Cinema de Luxe'* (*Y Neuadd Ddirwest gynt) yn dangos ffilm D.W. Griffith* Orphans of the Storm, *1921. Mae'r gofeb i filwyr Rhyfel De Affrica ar y chwith.*
The Cinema de Luxe (previously the Temperance Hall) showing D.W. Griffith's *Orphans of the Storm*, 1921. The South African War memorial stands on the left.

Y *'Carmarthen Arms' Cartlett, tua 1910. Mae Miss Morgan yn sefyll y tu allan gyda dau gwsmer.*
The Carmarthen Arms, Cartlett, *c*1910. Miss Morgan is standing outside with two customers.

Yr helfa yn ymgynnull y tu allan i'r Gwesty'r Castell, tua 1930.
A hunt gathers outside the Castle Hotel, c1930.

Y cŵn hela yn Scotchwell, Medi 1923.
Hounds gathered at Scotchwell, September 1923.

Aelodau o Dîm Pêl-droed Sefydliad y Dynion, Ebrill 1906.
Members of the Men's Institute Football Club, April 1906.

Aelodau o glwb Pêl-droed Eglwys y Santes Fair, 1912.
Members of St. Mary's Boys Football Club, 1912.

Rhyw ddefod ryfedd gan 'Brownies' Hwlffordd yng Nghastell Penfro, Mai 1939.
Haverfordwest Brownie Pack carrying out a strange ritual at Pembroke Castle, May 1939.

Sgowtiaid Eglwys Prendergast yn brecwasta yn y coed, 1910.
Prendergast Church Boy Scouts having breakfast in a wood, 1910.

A.J. Wright, Capten Brigâd y Bechgyn, yn Hwlffordd, yn 1917.
Captain of Haverfordwest Boys' Brigade, A. J. Wright, in 1917.

Yr Uwch-ringyll Edward Pearce, Sefydlydd a Hyfforddwr Mygedol Brigâd y Bechgyn, Hwlffordd, 1917.
Sgt-Major Edward Pearce, Founder and Honorary Instructor of Haverfordwest Boys' Brigade, 1917.

Sgowtiaid lleol yn cael te parti, 1910.
Local scouts enjoying tea and cake, 1910.

Côr Tabernacl ar daith i Dale. Cwmni Bland sydd â'r cerbydau a dynnid gan dri o geffylau ochr yn ochr.
Tabernacle Choir outing to Dale, 1912. The brakes were supplied by Bland's and were pulled by three horses abreast.

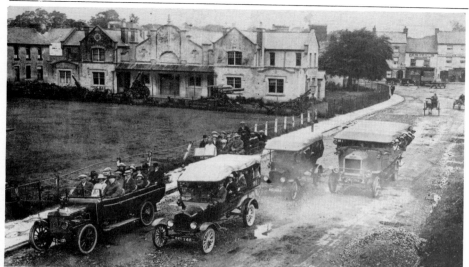

Nifer o gerbydau siarabang yn Heol Cartlett, tua 1920. Mae o leiaf un o'r cerbydau yn eiddo i Garej Green. Gellir gweld Gwaith Cerbydau a Moduron Bland yng nghornel uchaf y llun ar y dde, yn Sgwâr Pen-y-bont. Y tu hwnt i Erddi'r Jiwbili, ar y chwith, y mae'r Neuadd Ddril gydag amrywiaeth hynod o ddrylliau mawr olwynog o'i blaen.

Charabancs in Cartlett Road, c1920. At least one vehicle has been supplied by Green's Garage. Bland's Carriage and Motor Works may be seen, top right, in Bridge End Square. Beyond Jubilee Gardens, left, is the Drill Hall, with a remarkable array of gun carriages in front.

Y llong-ager Amy *yn derbyn teithwyr ar Gei y Gwaith Nwy, tua 1900.*
The river steamer *Amy* taking on passengers from the Gasworks Quay, c1900.

Côr Merched Hwlffordd, tua 1924. Yr arweinydd yw Mr W.J. Edwards; y gyfeilyddes yw Mrs W. Douglas Owen.

Haverfordwest Ladies' Choir, c1924. The conductor is Mr W.J. Edwards; the accompanist, Mrs W. Douglas Owen.

Côr Meibion Hwlffordd, tua 1908. Yr arweinydd yw Mr Adams.
Haverfordwest Male Voice Choir, c1908. The conductor is Mr Adams.

Cymdeithas Gorawl Hwlffordd y tu allan i Eglwys Gadeiriol Tyddewi adeg perfformio'r Messiah *gan Handel, ar Fehefin 12fed, 1924.*
Haverfordwest Choral Society outside St. David's Cathedral on the occasion of a performance of Handel's *Messiah*, 12 June 1924.

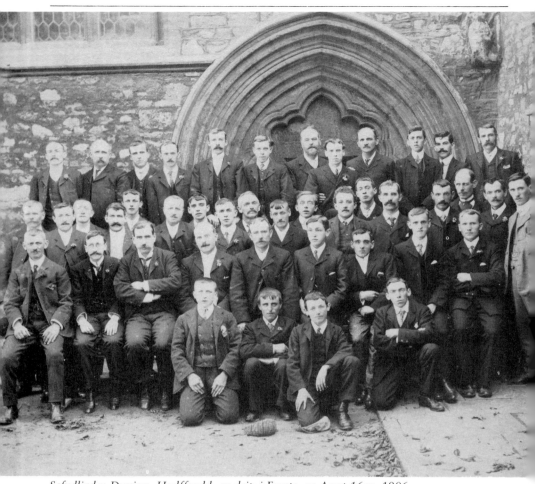

Sefydliad y Dynion, Hwlffordd, ar drip i Fryste, ar Awst 16eg, 1906.
Haverfordwest Men's Institute on a trip to Bristol, 16 August 1906.

Tai Nodedig
Notable Houses

Haylett Grange, tua 1908, pan oedd yn gartref i'r teulu Dawkins. Y pensaer oedd David Thomas, ac fe godwyd y tŷ tua 1890 i Sydney Dawkins.

Haylett Grange, c1908, when it was occupied by the Dawkins family. The architect was David Thomas and it was built c1890 for Sydney Dawkins.

Teulu yn cael te yn Llwynhelyg. Y foneddiges yn y gadair olwynog yw Martha, gweddw William Owen, 1884.

A family group at Withybush taking afternoon tea. The lady in the bath chair is Martha, William Owen's widow, 1884.

George Leader Owen, a dynnodd y rhan fwyaf o'r lluniau hyn o Llywnhelyg a'r trigolion yn gynnar yn yr 1880au. Roedd yn fab i William Owen, Poyston, a brynodd Llwynhelyg yn 1859.

George Leader Owen, who took most of these photographs of Withybush and its inhabitants in the early 1880s. He was the son of William Owen of Poyston, who bought Withybush in 1859.

Jane, y Fonesig Maxwell o Calderwood, gwraig George Leader Owen, ar gefn ceffyl, 1884.
Jane, Lady Maxwell of Calderwood, wife of George Leader Owen, on horseback, 1884.

Tynnwyd y llun hwn o'r ddwy ferch ifanc hyn yn Llwynhelyg gan George Leader Owen yn 1884.
These two young girls were photographed at Withybush by George Leader Owen in 1884.

Tŷ Llwynhelyg, 1884. Fe'i dymchwelyd i gael lle ar gyfer y maes glanio.
Withybush House, 1884. It was demolished to make way for the aerodrome.

Y tŷ, ychydig cyn ei ddymchwel.
The house, shortly before demolition.

Tŷ Cottesmore, fu unwaith yn gartref i'r teulu Massy, yn yr 1880au cynnar.
Cottesmore House, one-time home of the Massy family, in the early 1880s.

Tŷ Poyston yn yr 1880au. Mae'n dŷ annedd hyd heddiw; bu am flynyddoedd lawer ym meddiant Henry Owen, brawd George Leader Owen, a chyn hynny ym meddiant y teulu Picton.
Poyston House in the 1880s. Still occupied today, it belonged for many years to Henry Owen, the brother of George Leader Owen, and, before that, to the Picton family.

Gerddi Poyston, tua 1884, gyda dau o'r garddwyr ym mhen blaen y llun. O graffu ar y llun gellir gweld y teulu yn sefyll yng nghysgod y coed.
Poyston gardens, c1884, with two garden workers in the foreground. Closer examination shows the family all lined up under the trees.

Tŷ Scotchwell, yn gynnar yn yr ugeinfed ganrif. Fe'i hail-gynlluniwyd tua 1860 gan ddilyn sylfeini'r ddeunawfed ganrif. Ganed y Llyngesydd John Lort Stokes (1812–85) yno, a bu farw yno hefyd. Bu'n gwasanaethu gyda Darwin ar y Beagle, *a thrywanwyd ef â gwaywffon gan frodorion Awstralia. Cyhoeddwyd ei* Discoveries in Australia *ar ffurf dwy gyfrol yn 1846.*

Scotchwell House, early twentieth century. It was remodelled c1860 on an eighteenth-century core. Admiral John Lort Stokes (1812–85) was born and died here. He served with Darwin on the *Beagle* and was speared by Australian aborigines. His two-volume *Discoveries in Australia* was published in 1846.

Gât a Phorthordy Scotchwell, tua 1900.
Scotchwell Gate and Lodge, *c*1900.

*Avallenau, Pont Myrddin, a bensaerniwyd gan William Owen, pensaer lleol. Fe'i codwyd
yn 1845 ar gyfer William Evans, a enwodd y tŷ yn Avallenau, sef ffurf wedi'i Seisnigeiddio
ar 'Afallennau' sy'n golygu coed afalau.*

Avallenau, Merlins Bridge, designed by local architect William Owen. It was built in 1845
for William Evans who named the house after an anglicized spelling of the Welsh word for
apple trees.

Tŷ Foley, a bensaerniwyd gan John Nash yn 1794 ar gyfer Mr Richard Foley, brawd y Llyngesydd Syr Thomas Foley, un o swyddogion Nelson. Tynnwyd y llun ynghanol yr ugeinfed ganrif; mae gwedd y lle wedi gwella'n ddiweddar.

Foley House, designed by John Nash in 1794 for Mr Richard Foley, brother of Admiral Sir Thomas Foley, one of Nelson's officers. The photograph is from the mid-twentieth century; the appearance has recently been improved.

Tŷ Willesden, a godwyd gan Nicholas Roch, a fu farw yn 1786.
Willesden House, built by Nicholas Roch, who died in 1786.

Gazebo oddi ar Ffordd y Ddinas, yn yr 1970au mae'n debyg.
A gazebo off City Road, probably in the 1970s.

Diolchiadau
Acknowledgements

Casglwyd y deunydd ar gyfer y gyfrol hon gan yr aelodau canlynol o staff Adran Gwasanaethau Diwylliannol Cyngor Sir Dyfed, sy'n cynnwys Archifau, Llyfrgelloedd ac Amgueddfeydd:
This book was compiled by members of staff of the Cultural Services Department of Dyfed County Council. The department comprises Archives, Libraries and Museums and the following staff were directly involved:

Mary John • David Moore • Peter Simmonds •Corinne Streets

Diolch i'r holl uniglion sydd, dros y blynyddoedd, wedi rhoi neu fenthyca lluniau i'r Adran a diolch hefyd i'r unigolion a'r sefydliadau a enwir isod sydd wedi'n cynorthwyo trwy roi caniatâd i atgynhyrchu'r lluniau sydd yn eu meddiant:
In addition to thanking the numerous donors, who over the years have provided photographs for the department's collections, the assistance of those individuals and organizations who gave permission for the reproduction of photographs in their possession must be acknowledged. These include:

Richard and Pauline Burdon • Gerald Oliver • Roger Worsley

Microsoft® Windows XP

Professional
and Home Edition

Copyright - Editions ENI - July 2002
ISBN: 2-7460-1627-3
Orignal Edition: ISBN: 2-7460-1438-6

Editions ENI

BP 32125
44021 NANTES Cedex 1

Tél. : 02.51.80.15.15
Fax : 02.51.80.15.16

e-mail : editions@ediENI.com
http://www.editions-eni.com

Author: Béatrice DABURON
English edition by Adrienne TOMMY
Straight to the Point collection directed by Corinne HERVO

Foreword

The aim of this book is to let you find rapidly how to perform any task in the **Windows XP** operating system.

Each procedure is described in detail and illustrated so that you can put it into action easily.

The final pages are given over to an **index** of the topics covered and an **appendix** of emoticons.

The typographic conventions used in this book are as follows:

Type faces used for specific purposes:

bold	indicates the option to take in a menu or dialog box.
italic	is used for notes and comments.
[Ctrl]	represents a key from the keyboard; when two keys appear side by side, they should be pressed simultaneously.

Symbols indicating the content of a paragraph:

▓	an action to carry out (activating an option, clicking with the mouse...).
⇨	a general comment on the command in question.
✍🖱	a technique which involves the mouse.
⬡	a keyboard technique.
🗏	a technique which uses options from the menus.

⬚ WINDOWS XP

1.1	Overview	1
1.2	Managing windows	9
1.3	Users	12

⬚ EXPLORER/MY COMPUTER

2.1	Using Explorer views	26
2.2	Managing files and folders	35
2.3	Search Companion	47
2.4	Drives	52

⬚ MULTIMEDIA APPLICATIONS

3.1	Windows Movie Maker	55
3.2	Windows Media Player	69
3.3	Digital Photos	82

⬚ CONFIGURATION

4.1	Toolbars	86
4.2	Start menu	89
4.3	Interface	94

📖 SYSTEM AND COMMUNICATION

5.1	System tools	106
5.2	Installing	112
5.3	Windows Messenger 4.0	119
5.4	Networks and communication	127
5.5	Remote assistance	130
5.6	Remote Desktop	141

APENDIX

Emoticons 145

INDEX

Index 146

Windows XP

1.1 Overview

A-Starting Windows XP

▓ When you start up your computer, all its users appear by default in the Windows XP Welcome screen.

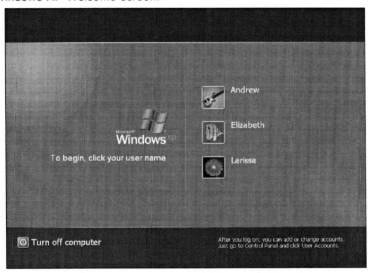

If you are the only user on your computer, the Welcome screen does not appear: Windows XP will open your working session automatically and you will go straight to the Windows desktop.

If several users have been created and you do not see the Windows XP Welcome screen, it means that this screen has been deactivated (Cf. 1.1 - B - Opening or activating a new work session). In this case, to log on to the computer, you must enter your user name, and any password you may have, in the Log On to Windows dialog box.

▓ As Windows prompts you to do, click your **user name** then if you have one, give your **password** to start your work session.

▓ If you forget your password, click the  button to see a hint to help you remember your password (cf. 1.3 - B - Managing a user password).

When you enter your password, each character appears as a dot.

When you have finished entering your password, click the button or press the ⌨Enter key to confirm.

B-Opening or activating a new work session

When Fast User Switching is active

This feature allows users to open several sessions simultaneously on the one computer. It is active by default.

To open another session, click the **start** button then **Log Off** (this is a misnomer, as you can also use it to activate a new session!).

Click the **Switch User** button 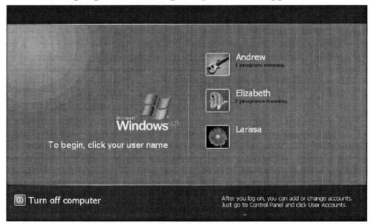 in the **Log Off Windows** dialog box to open the Windows Welcome screen (or the **Log Off Windows** dialog box, as the case may be).

From the Windows Welcome screen, the second user clicks his/her name to open a session and, if required, enters his/her password. From the **Log Off Windows** dialog box, he/she enters a user name and the associated password, if there is one, then clicks **OK**.

Windows does not close the previous session, it merely puts it "on hold". To reactivate it, click the **start** button then the **Log Off** button.

On the Windows Welcome screen, open sessions are indicated either by the number of programs running or by the text Logged on.

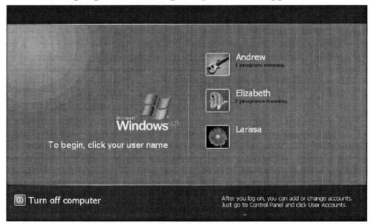

Each user can open only one session at a time.

Next, click the user whose session you want to reactivate.

⇨ *To open a session from the default Welcome screen (and not from the* ***Log Off Windows*** *dialog box), click the* ***start*** *button, take* ***Control Panel - User Accounts - Change the way users log on or off*** *and tick the* ***Use the Welcome screen*** *option. To use the dialog box, deactivate the same option.*

⇨ *The* ⊞ ***L*** *shortcut key can also be used to switch users.*

When Fast User Switching is not active

If Fast User Switching is inactive, you will have to close one session to open another.

▓ To open another session, click the **start** button then **Log Off**.

▓ Click the **Log Off** button.

▓ From the Windows Welcome screen, click the name of the user for whom you want to open a session and, if required, enter the password.
From the **Log Off Windows** dialog box, enter the user name and the password, if necessary, and click **OK**.

C-Closing a Windows XP session

▓ Click the **start** button then the 🔑 **Log Off** button.

▓ Click the **Log Off** button in the dialog box that appears.

▓ Windows closes all the open applications and checks when open files were last saved. If you have not saved the last changes you made to your files, Windows offers to do this: if this is the case, click **OK**.

Windows then saves your settings and opens the Welcome screen, which you can use to open a new session.

D-Discovering the Windows XP desktop

An example of a Windows XP desktop

▒ It contains:

- The **taskbar**: this makes it easier to access each task, or each open application. When you start your computer, the taskbar generally contains a **start** button, which you click to display the main Windows menu. At the right of the taskbar, you can see the **notification area**, containing the clock and specific icons alerting you to an event (such as incoming e-mail).
- Various other objects symbolised by icons may appear on the desktop: the **Recycle Bin** is there to receive any files you delete.
  Other objects, such as shortcuts to applications or files, may also appear on the desktop.

▒ If you point to the time shown on the taskbar, your computer's control date will appear.

Using the start button

*This button opens the customized **start** menu, which carries the name of its associated user.*

▒ Click the **start** button or press the ⊞ key or $\boxed{\text{Ctrl}}\boxed{\text{Esc}}$ on your keyboard to open the **start** menu.

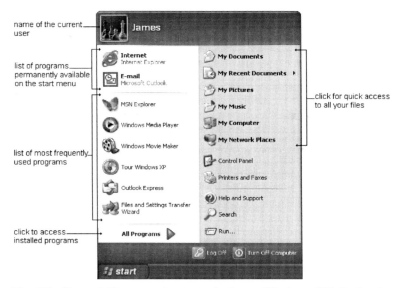

name of the current user

list of programs permanently available on the start menu

list of most frequently used programs

click to access installed programs

click for quick access to all your files

The **My Recent Documents** menu (only on Windows XP Professional) contains a list of the last 15 files you used.

The **My Documents** button displays all your work items filed into three folders: **My Music**, **My Videos** and **My Pictures** (the **My Videos** subfolder is generated automatically when you start the Windows Movie Maker application).

The **My Pictures** and **My Music** buttons display the content of the corresponding folders.

The **My Computer** button provides access to all the components of your computer.

The **Control Panel** button opens a window of the same name that you can use to modify your working environment.

The **Printers and Faxes** button (on Windows XP Professional) activates a window of the same name, to add a printer, set up faxing and so on.

The **Help and Support** button provides access to the Windows XP **Help and Support Center** application.

The **Search** button provides access to a number of options for finding files, folders or people (in an address book) or for searching the Internet.

The **Run** button can be used to run a program by specifying the corresponding executable file.

The **Log Off** button closes the current session and allows another user to log on.

The **Turn Off Computer** button should be activated before you switch off your computer.

⇨ *To close the start menu, click anywhere on the desktop or press the* Esc *button as many times as required.*

⇨ *To sort the **All Programs** list in alphabetical order, open the list, right-click it and choose the **Sort by Name** option.*

E-Starting an application

▨ Open the **start** menu, then in the **All Programs** list or the list of frequently used programs, click the name of the required application once.

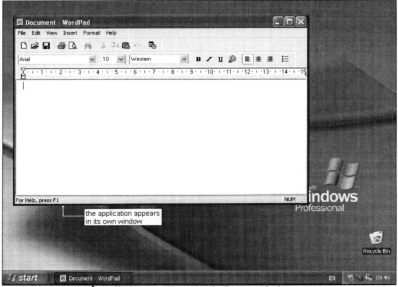

the application appears in its own window

└ a taskbar button appears, representing the open application

⇨ *If a shortcut appears on the taskbar, a simple click on the shortcut will open the application. If a shortcut exists on the desktop, double-click the shortcut to open the application.*

⇨ *If you encounter a problem with a program that worked correctly under your previous version of Windows, you can use the **Program Compatibility Wizard (start - All Programs - Accessories)** to try and solve the problem.*

⇨ *Some games or applications work better on a 256 colour display and/or in a screen resolution of 640 x 480. If this is the case, you can change these settings temporarily. To do this, right-click the game or program in the **start** menu then take the **Properties** option. Activate the **Compatibility** tab then tick the option(s) in the **Display settings** frame that corre-spond to the feature you wish to modify. Click **OK** to confirm. Start the game or program again. It is useful to know that the previous screen resolution and the default colour display quality will be restored once you close the program or game in question. The **Compatibility** tab is available only for applications installed on your hard disk and not for those on floppy disk, CD-ROM or the network.*

F- Leaving an application

░ This action closes the application window:

File Alt F4
Exit

░ If required, save the last changes made to the active file.

░ If the application window is minimized, right-click the corresponding taskbar button and choose **Close**.

G- Using Windows help

░ Open the **start** menu and activate the **Help and Support** option, or press F1.

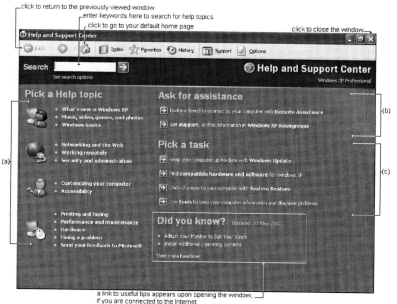

(a) To see the help topics for one of these categories, click the corresponding link.

(b) To use an external support feature, such as remote assistance, click one of these links.

(c) To get help on a certain task, look in the **Pick a task** list; you may find a link that refers to what you are looking for.

Finding help by using keywords

░ Click in the **Search** box, then enter the keywords that you want to use for your search.

░ Confirm your entry with the Enter key or click the button.

The Stop button stops the search in progress.

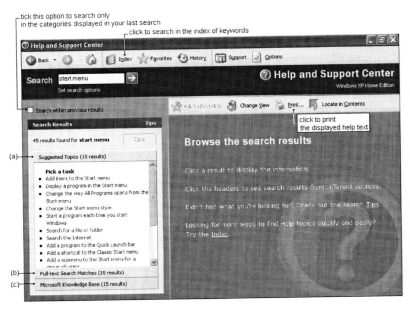

To show/hide one of the result groups, click its button:

Suggested Topics (a) list the results that are likely to be the most relevant: to produce this list Windows compares the words you entered with the keywords associated with its help documents.

Full-text Search Matches (b) list documents that contain the text you entered, but not necessarily as their keywords.

Be aware that if you use Windows XP Home Edition, it will supply full text search matches only if no **Suggested Topics** keyword results are found.

If you have an open Internet connection, Windows will search the Microsoft Knowledge Base Web site (c) (you will not see this happening).

H-Turning off the computer

Close all the current sessions click the **start** button then click the **Turn Off Computer** button.

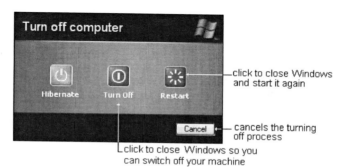

—click to close Windows and start it again

—cancels the turning off process

└click to close Windows so you can switch off your machine

▓ Depending on your computer, it will either turn itself off automatically after a brief pause or Windows will tell you that you can switch off the power (on some computers, you may need to hold the main unit's power button pressed in for a few moments before the power will switch off).

1.2 Managing windows

A-Description of a window

▓ Each window contains the following items:

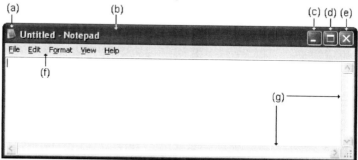

- the **Control** menu button (a), which you can use to manage the size and position of the window or to close it.

- a **title bar** (b), which reminds you of the name of the active file (here, this is called **Untitled** as the current file has not yet been saved and named) followed by the name of the application.

- the **Minimize** (c) and **Maximize** (d) buttons: the first reduces the window to a button on the taskbar and the second expands the window to fill the whole screen.

- the **Close** button (e), which you use to close the window and leave the application.
- the **menu bar** (f) contains the application's various menus (these are closed in the illustration). Use the **Help** menu to get help on the application.
- the **scroll bars and arrows** (g) are used to scroll the contents of the window (here they appear dim because the window is empty).

B-Moving a window

▦ Point to the window's title bar.

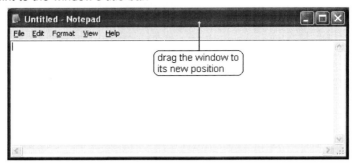

C-Resizing a window

▦ To enlarge a window so that it takes up the whole screen, click the ▣ button on the window's title bar.

The window fills the screen. Only the taskbar is still visible (although you can hide this too if you wish).

▦ To restore the window to its previous size, click the ▣ button.

▦ To change the width or height of a window, point to the appropriate edge of the window: to change the width and height of a window, point to one of its corners. Drag the pointer to resize the window.

▦ To remove the window from the screen without shutting the application, click the ▬ button, or click the taskbar button that corresponds to the application.

▦ To open one of the windows shown on the taskbar, simply click its button.

D-Managing several windows

▨ When two windows overlap, you can recognise the active window by its darker title bar. The corresponding button on the taskbar will also appear pressed in.

▨ To access a window and activate that application, click the window if it is visible, or if not, click the corresponding button on the taskbar.

The active window appears in the foreground.

You can also press the [Alt][⇄] *shortcut key until the required application window is activated.*

▨ To change the layout of the windows, right-click any empty space on the taskbar to display the bar's shortcut menu then choose one of these options:

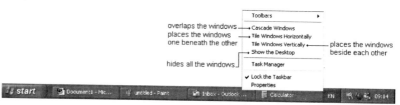

▨ To show all the windows again, if you reduced them with the **Show the Desktop** option, display the taskbar shortcut menu then use **Undo Minimize All** or **Show Open Windows**.

E-Closing a window

▨ Click the ❌ button on the window or press the [Alt][F4] keys, if you are closing an application window or [Ctrl][F4] if you are closing a document window.

⇨ *Closing an application window means that you shut down that application: if the application contains an open, unsaved file, Windows will offer to save that file before closing the application.*

⇨ *In an application window, you can also use the* **File - Exit** *command to close the application.*

1.3 Users

A-Adding a user to your computer

To add a user account, you must log on as a Computer administrator.

▨ Click the **start** button then **Control Panel** - **User Accounts** - **Create a new account**.

▨ Enter a user name in the **Type a name for the new user** box then click **Next**.

① Define the type of account required for the new user, by choosing the appropriate option.

② Confirm the account.

B-Managing a user password

While a Computer administrator can make any changes he or she wants to the user accounts, a Limited user can carry out only certain changes.

If you use Windows XP Professional, you will be able to carry out the features described below only if your computer was defined as a member of a workgroup and not as a member of a domain when Windows XP was first installed.

Depending on the version of Windows XP you are using (Professional or Home Edition), the option names or titles on your computer may differ slightly from those described in this chapter.

Associating a password with a user

▨ Open the **User Accounts** dialog box (**start - Control Panel - User Accounts**).

▨ If you are logged on as the Computer administrator, click the name of the user to whom you want to give a password in the **or pick an account to change** list (this can be your own account).

If you are using a Limited type of account, you will not be able to access other user accounts: your own will be activated automatically.

Click **Create a password**.

*If you are creating a password for your own account, this window will be called **Create a password for your account**.*

① Enter the password once in this box (a), then confirm it in this box (b). Be careful: Windows differentiates between upper and lower case letters!

② To enter a hint in case of a forgotten password, click this box and enter a word or phrase to remind you of your password.

③ Confirm the password.

If you are logged on as the Computer administrator, Windows XP will ask if you want to make your files and folders private:

click to prevent other users from accessing ──┘
your files/folders (despite the password protection)

⇨ *To display the password hint when you are entering the password in the Windows XP Welcome screen, click the ❓ button.*

Changing the password

▨ Open the **User Accounts** dialog box.

▨ If you are logged on as the Computer administrator, click the name of the user whose password you wish to modify in the **or pick an account to change** list (this can be your own account).

If you are using a Limited type of account, your own account will be activated automatically.

▨ Click the **Change my password** link (if you are changing your own account) or **Change the password** (if you are working on someone else's account).

▨ In the **Type your current password** box, enter the password needed to open the session.

▨ To enter a new password, click the **Type a new password** box and enter the new password then click the **Type the new password again to confirm** box and enter the password a second time.

▨ To enter a password hint, click the **Type a word or phrase to use as a password hint** box and give the required text.

Changing the password erases the old password hint automatically. If you wish to keep the same password hint, you will have to enter it again.

▨ Click the **Change Password** button.

Deleting a password

▨ Open the **User Accounts** dialog box.

▨ If you are logged on as the Computer administrator, click the name of the user whose password you wish to remove in the **or pick an account to change** list (this can be your own account).

If you are using a Limited type of account, your account will be activated automatically.

▨ Click the **Remove my password** or **Remove the password** link as appropriate.

▨ If you are removing a password for an account other than the active one, Windows XP reminds you of the consequences of removing the password:

Are you sure you want to remove Ruth's password?

You are removing the password for Ruth. **If you do this, Ruth will lose all EFS-encrypted files, personal certificates, and stored passwords for Web sites or network resources.**

Also, if you remove this password, other people can gain access to Ruth's account and change settings.

To avoid losing data in the future, ask Ruth to make a password reset floppy disk.

[Remove Password]   [Cancel]

▨ If you want to delete your own password, Windows reminds you what effect this will have and asks you to identify yourself:

Are you sure you want to remove your password?

If you remove your password, other people can gain access to your account and change settings.

To verify your identity, type your current password:

Show password hint

[Remove Password]   [Cancel]

▨ Once you have read this message and, if necessary, entered the password to identify yourself, click the **Remove Password** button.

C-Using a password reset disk

This technique saves your password information on a floppy disk, so that, if you forget the password, you can access your files again.

Creating a password reset disk

To use this feature, you must be logged on to the user account for which you wish to create the disk.

▨ Open the **User Accounts** dialog box.

If you are logged on as the Computer administrator, click your user name in the or pick an account to change list.

If you are using a Limited type of account, your own account will be activated automatically.

- Click the **Prevent a forgotten password** link in the left pane of the window.
- Click the **Next** button on the **Forgotten Password Wizard** dialog box.
- Insert a blank floppy disk into the disk drive.
- Click the **Next** button.

└ enter the current password and click Next

- When Windows has finished copying the data, click the **Next** button then **Finish**.

⇨ *Make sure you keep this disk in a safe place, known only to yourself!*

If you lose your password

If you forget your password, you can still log on using the password reset disk you created earlier.

- In the Windows Welcome screen, select your user name and click the button.

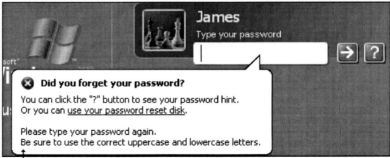

└ this message can appear only if a password reset disk has been created for this user

- Click the **use your password reset disk** link.
- Click the **Next** button on the **Password Reset Wizard**.
- Insert the reset disk into the floppy disk drive and click **Next**.
- Enter your new password in the password box then enter it a second time in the **Type the password again to confirm** box.
- If you wish, **Type a new password hint** in the appropriate box and click the **Next** button.
- Click the **Finish** button in the **Completing the Password Reset Wizard** window.
- Take the floppy disk out of the drive and put it in a safe place.

You can re-use this disk, should you ever forget your password again. You do not need to recreate a new disk each time.

⇨ *If you lose your password reset disk or if you did not create one, ask your Administrator to create a new password for you. For security reasons, an administrator cannot restore a lost password but only create a new one. Once you are able to log on again, remember to create a reset disk!*

D-Managing user accounts

- Open the **User Accounts** dialog box.

Changing a user name

Only the Computer administrator can use this feature.

- Click the user name that you wish to modify, then click the **Change the name** link (or **Change my name** if you are working on your own user account).
- In the **Type a new name for (user)** box, enter or modify the required user name.
- Click the **Change Name** button to confirm.

Changing a user's picture

- If you are logged on as the Computer administrator, click the user name concerned in the list.

If you are using a Limited type of account, your account will be activated automatically.

- Click the **Change the picture** link (or **Change my picture** if you are working on your account).

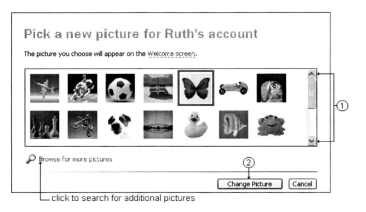

① Click the picture you wish to use to illustrate the chosen account.

② Confirm your choice.

Changing the user account type

Only the Computer administrator can use this feature.

▓ Click the user name whose account type you wish to modify.

▓ Click the **Change the account type** link (or **Change my account type** if you are working on your own account).

▓ Activate the required account type (**Computer administrator** or **Limited**) then click the **Change Account Type** button.

Deleting a user account

Only the Computer administrator can use this feature.

▓ Click the user name whose account you wish to delete, then click the **Delete the account** link.

The active administrator cannot delete his/her own account.

(a)   Click here to delete the account along with its files and folders.

(b)   Click here to delete the account, but keep the user's files and folders.

▓ When Windows asks you to confirm deleting the account (and the files and folders if you requested this), click the **Delete Account** button.

E-Activating/deactivating the Guest account

To use this feature, you must be logged on as the Computer administrator.

▓ Open the **User Accounts** dialog box.

▓ Click the **Guest** user name, then click the **Turn On the Guest Account** button (if the account is not active) or the **Turn off the guest account** link (if the Guest account is active).

F-Activating/deactivating Fast User Switching

To use this feature, you must be logged on as the Computer administrator.

▓ Open the **User Accounts** dialog box.

▓ Click the **Change the way users log on or off** link.

▓ Tick the **Use Fast User Switching** check box if you want programs being used by one user to remain open while another user logs on, or deactivate this option if you want programs to close when there is a change of user.

▓ Click the **Apply Options** button.

⇨ *You should not deactivate this option while several sessions are open.*

⇨ *This option is inaccessible if the Use the Welcome screen option in the same dialog box is not active.*

G-Protecting your personal folders

By making them private

To prevent other users from accessing your personal folders (My Documents and its subfolders, your personal desktop, start menu, cookies and Favorites), you should make them private.

▓ Click the **start** button followed by **My Computer**.

▓ Double-click the hard disk drive on which Windows is installed.

▓ Double-click the **Documents and Settings** folder then your user folder.

▓ Right-click the folder you want to protect then click the **Properties** option.

▓ Click the **Sharing** tab then tick the **Make this folder private** check box. Click **OK** to confirm.

For this feature to be available, your hard disk must have been formatted as NTFS.

By encrypting them

To prevent other users, including Computer administrators, from accessing your files, you can encrypt them. This feature is available only to users of Windows XP Professional whose hard disk or partition is formatted as NTFS.

- Click the **start** button then **My Computer**.
- To select a particular file or folder, double-click your personal folder in the **Files Stored on This Computer** list then click the folder or file you want to encrypt.
  To encrypt all of your personal folders, click its name in the **Files Stored on This Computer** list.
- Right-click the file or folder you wish to encrypt and choose the **Properties** option.
- Click the **Advanced** button in the **Attributes** frame on the **General** page.
- Tick the **Encrypt contents to secure data** option then click the **OK** button.
- Click **OK** on the **Properties** dialog box.
  The dialog box may vary depending on whether you are encrypting a file or a folder.
- If you are encrypting a folder:

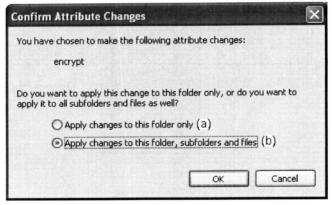

- Activate option (a) to encrypt only the selected folder and not its subfolders, or option (b) to encrypt the selected folder along with all its subfolders and files.

If you are encrypting just a selected file:

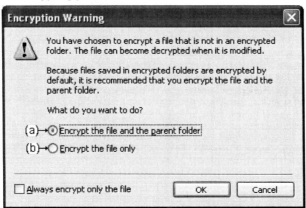

Activate option (a) to encrypt only the selected file or (b) to encrypt the selected file and the folder containing it.

Click the **OK** button to confirm.

*The encrypted files/folders appear in a different colour (green) in the Windows Explorer and in My Computer, providing the **Show encrypted or compressed NTFS files in colour** option has been ticked in **My Computer - Tools - Folder Options - View** tab.*

⇨ *You cannot compress (or zip) and encrypt the same file or folder. If you encrypt a folder by itself or with its subfolders and files, any files or subfolders added subsequently to that folder will be encrypted automa- tically.*

⇨ *To decrypt a folder and/or file, deactivate the **Encrypt contents to secure data** option in the **Advanced Attributes** dialog box.*

H-Creating a Microsoft .NET Passport

If you already have an account with MSN Explorer or Hotmail, this account will act as a passport.

Open the **User Accounts** dialog box.

If you are logged on as a Computer administrator, click your user name in the **or pick an account to change** list.

If you are logged on as a Limited user, your account is active automatically.

Click the **Set up my account to use a .NET Passport** link.

Windows suggests either that you use your existing e-mail address for your new Passport or that you create an MSN.com account (and a Hotmail.com e-mail address) to use for your Passport.

You want to create an MSN.com account

▨ In the second **.NET Passport Wizard** screen (**Do you have an e-mail address**), activate the **No, I would like to open a free MSN.com e-mail account now** option and click **Next**.

▨ Enter your **First Name** then your **Last Name** and click the **Next** button.

▨ In the **Where do you live?** dialog box, fill in the **Country/Region, State, Zip Code** and **Time Zone** boxes then click the **Next** button.

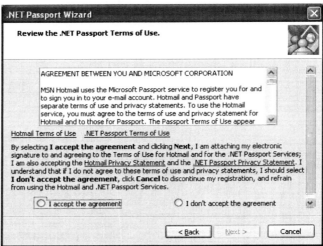

▨ Read the .NET Passport terms of use then activate the **I accept the agreement** option and click **Next** to continue creating the account.

▨ In the next dialog box, fill in the **Birth Date, Gender** and **Occupation** boxes then click the **Next** button.

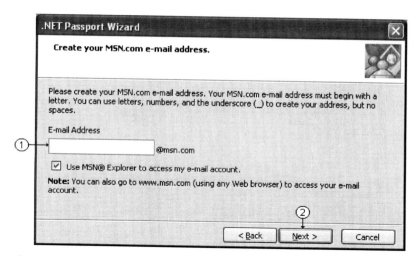

① Enter the name you wish to use for the e-mail address, respecting the constraints detailed in the dialog box.

② Click this button to continue.

▨ Enter a **Password** for your account then confirm your password by entering it again in the **Retype Password** box.

Your password must contain at least six characters: it can contain uppercase and lowercase letters, numbers and standard symbols. It must not contain spaces, extended characters or the name part of your e-mail address.

▨ Click the **Next** button.

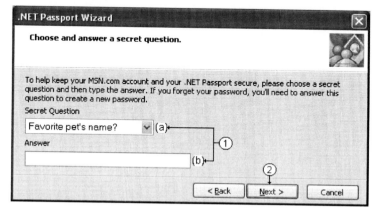

① In case you lose your password, Windows XP asks you to choose a secret question in list (a) and to give your personal answer in list (b). By doing this, if ever you forget your password and want to create a new one, you will have to give the exact answer to your question to be identified.

② Click to continue the procedure.

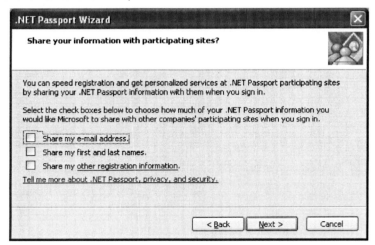

▓ When you visit sites using .NET Passport, you can choose to let these sites know your e-mail address, your first and last names and/or other registration information that was used to set up your passport. This means you avoid filling in this information every time. If you want to do this, tick the appropriate options and click **Next**.

▓ To be listed in the **Hotmail Member Directory**, activate the corresponding option then click the **Next** button.

Windows tells you that your Windows XP account can now use the .NET Passport you have just created.

▓ Click **Finish** to confirm creating your passport.

You want to use your existing e-mail address for your Passport

▓ In the second **.NET Passport Wizard** screen (**Do you have an e-mail address**) (cf. page 22), activate the **Yes** option.

▓ Click the **Next** button.

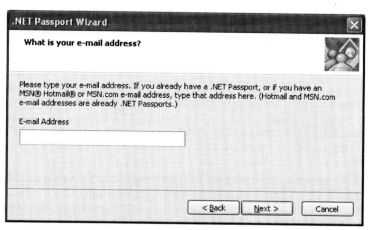

- Enter your **E-mail Address** in the text box then click **Next**.
- If you enter a Hotmail or MSN.com e-mail address, Windows asks you to enter your password for this account.
- If you do not enter a Hotmail or MSN.com e-mail address, enter a **Password** for your account then confirm your password by entering it again.
- Carry on creating your Passport account as described in the **You want to create an MSN.com account** section.

2.1 Using Explorer views

A- Opening the Windows Explorer

Whether or not you are authorised to carry out certain tasks will depend on whether you are the Computer administrator, a Limited user or a Guest.

▓ **start** - **All Programs** - **Accessories** - **Windows Explorer**

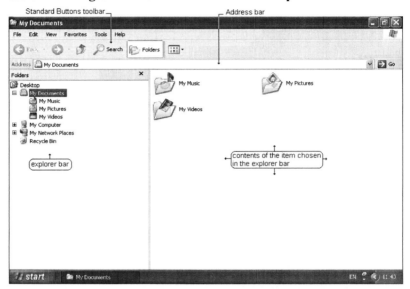

There are five different explorer bars. When you open the Windows Explorer, the **Folders** *explorer bar opens by default.*

▓ To show or hide the **Status Bar**, activate or deactivate the corresponding option in the **View** menu (it is deactivated by default).

▓ To show or hide a toolbar, activate or deactivate the corresponding option in **View - Toolbars**.

▓ To hide the explorer bar, click the ☒ button at the top of it. To reactivate the **Folders** explorer bar, click the 📁 Folders button.

⇨ *You can also start the Windows Explorer by right-clicking the* **start** *button and choosing the* **Explore** *option: this takes you to the active user's* **Start Menu** *folder. Choose the* **Explore All Users** *button to go to the* **Start Menu** *folder in the* **All Users** *folder (only the Computer administrator can see this last option).*

B-Using the Folders bar

The different elements on the desktop are displayed as a tree: some branches of the tree (a) are expanded (displaying a - sign), to show the objects and folders they contain; others (b) are collapsed (displaying a + sign), to hide their contents. To expand or collapse a branch, click the + or - sign.

To see what an item contains (a disk, drive or folder), click that item.

To expand a branch completely, click the branch then press *.

To see the contents of a folder, click that folder.

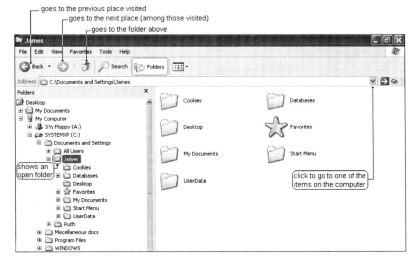

⇨ *To update the contents of the window (if changes have been made since you displayed it) use the **View - Refresh** command or* F5 .

⇨ *You can also display the Folders bar by using the **View - Explorer Bar - Folders** command.*

C-Using the History bar

▓ **View - Explorer Bar - History** or Ctrl **H**

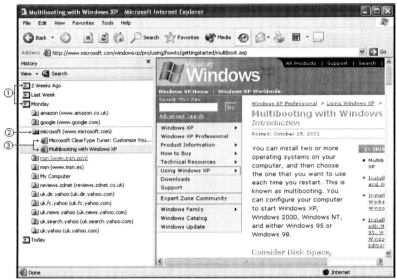

① To see the files opened on a specific day or week, click that day or week.

② Click the <u>site</u> containing the pages that you want to see.

③ To see an HTML page in the right pane of the screen, click its name.

▓ To modify how History items are listed in the bar, click the **View** button on the bar, then specify whether the pages should be listed **By Date**, **By Site**, **By Most Visited** or **By Order Visited Today**.

▓ To search within the History bar, click the ▓ Search button.

① Enter the start of the name or the whole name of the page you wish to find.

② Click to start the search.

▓ To close the **Search** pane of the History explorer bar, click the **View** button and choose a view type for the bar.

D-Using the Favorites bar

▓ **View - Explorer Bar - Favorites** or ⌨Ctrl⌨ I

▓ To go to one of the Web pages listed in the Favorites, click the name of the folder (and subfolder, if appropriate) containing the Web page you want to see then click that page's name.

The page's address appears in the Address Bar.

▓ To add a Web page to the Favorites folder, enter the Web page's address in the **Address Bar**, then press the ⌨Enter⌨ key.

The page's contents appear in the right hand side of the screen.

▓ **Favorites**
 Add to Favorites

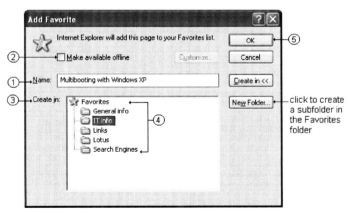

click to create a subfolder in the Favorites folder

① Enter the name of the page.

② Activate this option if you wish to be able to consult the page offline.

③ Click the **Create in >>** button to open this frame.

④ Specify where you wish to save the Web page.

⑤ Click to confirm.

▨ To organize the Favorites folder, use **Favorites - Organize Favorites** or ⬚ Organize...

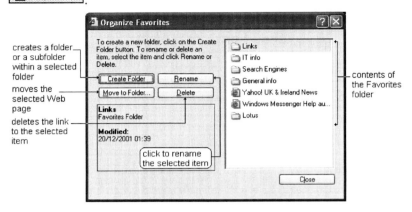

E- Using the Media bar

▨ **View - Explorer Bar - Media**

For a short while, Windows looks for various pieces of information on the WindowsMedia.com site:

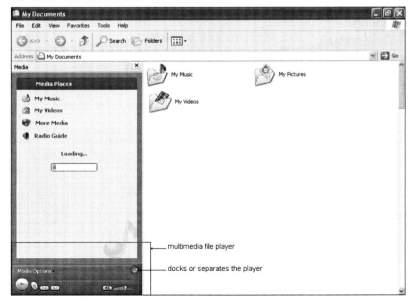

*If your Internet connection is offline, a message will ask you to **Go back to the previous menu**. Click this link to return to the page presented above.*

▦ From this pane, click one of the folders offered (such as **My Music** or **My Videos**) to open it. Next, click the file you want to see in the right pane of the window.

▦ Start playing the audio or video file using the ⊙ button on the player.

If you are playing a video, a small screen appears above the play bar.

Windows Movie Maker Sample File.wmv

└click to stop playing the file

If your Internet connection is online, Windows XP offers you multimedia news, found on the WindowsMedia.com site:

■ Click **Media Options** on the player and choose an option:

Radio Guide   to see a list of radio sites. To listen to one of the stations, click the corresponding link.

More Media   to display the WindowsMedia.com site, from which you can see film trailers or listen to music or radio.

▷ *If you want to read one of the audio or video files stored on your computer while your Internet connection is online, display those files with the Folders bar <u>before</u> activating the Media bar.*

F- Using the Search bar

■ **View**
Explorer Bar
Search

Ctrl E

*The **Search Companion** pane can be used to search for files, folders and items using the criteria you specify (cf. 2.3 - A - Using the Search Companion).*

G-Modifying how the list of folders/files is displayed

■ To change the view of the files/folder list, open the **View** menu or click

the button.

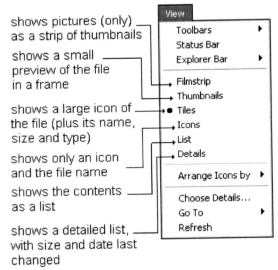

shows pictures (only) as a strip of thumbnails

shows a small preview of the file in a frame

shows a large icon of the file (plus its name, size and type)

shows only an icon and the file name

shows the contents as a list

shows a detailed list, with size and date last changed

*When you choose a **Details** layout, the list appears like this:*

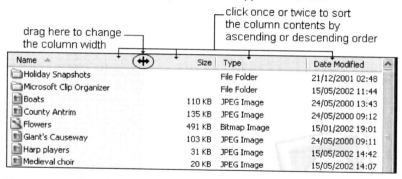

click once or twice to sort the column contents by ascending or descending order

drag here to change the column width

Name ▲	Size	Type	Date Modified
Holiday Snapshots		File Folder	21/12/2001 02:48
Microsoft Clip Organizer		File Folder	15/05/2002 11:44
Boats	110 KB	JPEG Image	24/05/2000 13:43
County Antrim	135 KB	JPEG Image	24/05/2000 09:12
Flowers	491 KB	Bitmap Image	15/01/2002 19:01
Giant's Causeway	103 KB	JPEG Image	24/05/2000 09:11
Harp players	31 KB	JPEG Image	15/05/2002 14:42
Medieval choir	20 KB	JPEG Image	15/05/2002 14:07

▓ To group the files displayed by name, size, type, date or time of modification, make sure you are in **Thumbnails**, **Icons** or **Details** view then open
the **View** menu. Point to the **Arrange Icons by** option and choose the
Show in Groups option. To change the type of grouping, open the **View**
menu again, choose **Arrange Icons by** and click one of the groups
offered (the active grouping is preceded by a dot).

⇨ *In **Details** layout, you can choose different columns to show with **View -
Choose Details**.*

H-Showing an image preview

▓ Go to the folder of pictures concerned.
▓ Activate the **Filmstrip** view in the **View** menu or use ▢.
▓ Click the image concerned in the strip of pictures.

shows the picture selected in the filmstrip

click to see the image to the right or left

rotates the image

Blue hills   Sunset   Water lilies   Winter

filmstrip of miniature pictures

EXPLORER/MY COMPUTER

▓ To print an image, right-click the image concerned and choose the **Print** option.

*The **Photo Printing Wizard** opens and guides you.*

I- Setting the folder view options

▓ **Tools - Folder Options**

▓ Activate the **View** tab.

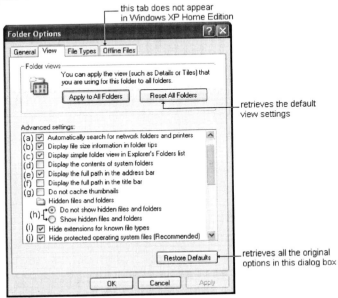

this tab does not appear
in Windows XP Home Edition

retrieves the default
view settings

retrieves all the original
options in this dialog box

▓ When you activate the following options:

(a)   Windows searches automatically for shared folders and printers and stores them in My Network Places.

(b)   Windows Explorer displays the size of the folder in the ScreenTip that appears when you point to a folder in the right hand pane.

(c)   The Explorer shows the full contents of a folder when you click it and closes all other folders.

(d)   Windows shows the files that your computer system needs to work correctly.

(e)   The full file path appears in the Address Bar.

(f)   The full file path appears in the title bar.

(g)   Windows will no longer memorise thumbnails it has made for image files.

(h)   Tick the appropriate option to hide/show hidden files.

(i)   Windows will not show extensions on file types it recognises.

(j)   Windows hides any operating system files within the folder in question to prevent unintended changes.

2.2 Managing files and folders

A-An overview of personal folders

▦ For each user of your computer, Windows XP creates an individual folder called **My Documents**, which contains two specialised subfolders by default: **My Pictures** and **My Music**.

▦ If you wish, you can allow other computer users to access your personal folder and its subfolders or you can make these folders private.

▦ If several users can access your computer, Windows XP identifies the different personal folders according to the name of the user concerned. For example, when James is logged on to the computer, his personal folder is called **My Documents**, (except in My Computer where it is called **James's Documents**) while Ruth's personal folder appears as **Ruth's Documents**. Windows identifies subfolders in the same way, for example the **My Pictures** folder becomes **Ruth's Pictures**.

▦ Windows XP also provides a **Shared Documents** folder for files that you wish to share with other users of the computer. The **Shared Documents** folder contains subfolders called **Shared Pictures** and **Shared Music**.

▦ Each user can create his or her own folders and subfolders at leisure.

▦ To get a better understanding of the Windows hierarchy, open the Windows Explorer (**start - All Programs - Accessories - Windows Explorer**):

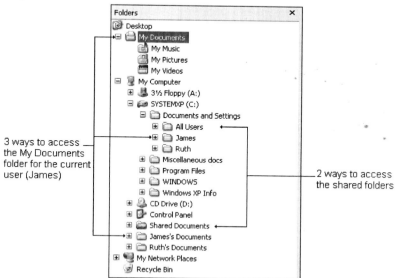

3 ways to access the My Documents folder for the current user (James)

2 ways to access the shared folders

⇨ *A quick way to access the **My Documents** folder is to click the link of the same name in the **start** menu.*

B-Managing file and folder selection

▒ To select files/folders, point to the empty space just to the right of the first name you wish to select. Drag the mouse until all the required names/icons are enclosed in a dotted rectangle.

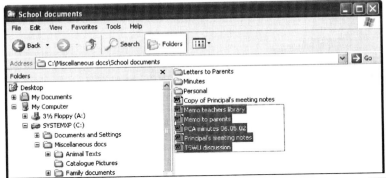

▒ To expand the selection to include adjacent files, hold down the ⇧ Shift key and click the last document you wish to include.

▒ To select another group of files, hold down ⇧ Shift and drag around the new group.

▒ To insert another file into the selection, hold down the Ctrl key and click the file you want to add.

▒ To select all the files in the active folder, use **Edit - Select All** or Ctrl **A**.

▒ To deselect selected files, hold down Ctrl and drag around the files you want to remove from the selection.

▒ To cancel all the current selection, click anywhere in the window (except on a file name!).

⇨ *You can also invert an existing selection (deselecting the current selection and selecting the rest of the files in the folder) with the Edit - Invert Selection command.*

⇨ *When a selection has been made, right-click the selection to see a shortcut menu, with options adapted to that selection.*

⇨ *You can also select via the keyboard: go to the first file, hold down* ⇧ Shift *then use the arrow keys to spread out the selection. To select a non-adjacent file, hold down* Ctrl *then use the* ⬆ *or* ⬇ *keys to go to it and* space *to select it.*

C-Creating a folder

▒ **start - My Documents**

▒ To create a subfolder of an existing folder double click the folder concerned. To create a folder in your **My Documents** folder (on the same level as **My Music** and **My Pictures**) do not select any folder or file in the **My Documents** window.

- Click the **Make a new folder** link in the left-hand pane (if the options of this box are not visible, click the ⓥ button first). If you do not have this link, you must have already selected a folder or file. Deselect this folder or file by clicking in a blank area of white space in the right-hand pane.

  Alternatively, right-click an empty space in the list, and choose the option **New** *then* **Folder***.*

- Enter the new folder's name (up to 255 characters long, including spaces, and not containing the characters \ / ?: * " < > or |).
- Press ⌈Enter⌋ to confirm.

D-Copying folders or files

First method

- If necessary, open the subfolder containing the item(s) you want to copy.
- In the right pane of the window, select the folders or files to be copied.
- Click the **Copy this file** link in the left pane.

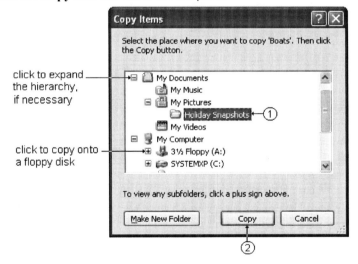

click to expand the hierarchy, if necessary

click to copy onto a floppy disk

① Click the name of the destination folder for the copied item(s).

② Click to confirm the copy.

Second method

- **View - Explorer Bar - Folders** or 🗁 Folders
- Select the folders or files concerned.
- Copy these documents into the clipboard: **Edit - Copy** or ⌈Ctrl⌋ **C**
- In the **Folders** bar, select the folder into which you wish to transfer the file/folder you copied into the clipboard.

░ Paste in the contents of the clipboard: **Edit - Paste** or Ctrl **V**.

The files are copied one by one. They are still in the clipboard so you can copy them to another location if you wish.

Third method

░ Display the **Folders** explorer bar and select the files or folders you want to copy.

░ Make sure the destination folder is accessible in the hierarchy (if it is a subfolder of another folder, the parent folder should be open).

░ Drag the files or folders to the destination folder. If you are copying onto the same drive, hold down the Ctrl key while you drag.

When you are dragging to copy, a + sign is attached to the mouse pointer.

⇨ *When you copy a folder, Windows copies the folder's entire hierarchy including any subfolders and files they may contain.*

⇨ *When the destination folder already contains a file with the same name as the one being copied, Windows will want to replace the first file (but it will ask you to confirm that first!).*

⇨ *If you copy a file into the folder containing the original, Windows creates a duplicate called Copy of... followed by the original file name.*

⇨ *If you are copying onto a network drive that does not support long file names, you will be asked to confirm that the first eight characters of the name can be used as the name of the destination file.*

E-Copying a file or folder onto a CD-ROM

The technique is simple: first you select the files you wish to copy. The selection is placed in a temporary file. When the list is ready, you can start writing to the CD-ROM.

Preparing the CD writer and your computer

░ Insert a blank CD-R or CD-RW into the writer then use **start** button - **My Computer**.

░ Click the CD writer icon.

░ **File - Properties** (or right-click the writer icon and choose **Properties**).

░ On the **General** page, check the available **Free space** on the CD.

A traditional CD has a capacity of 650 megabytes (MB), although there are extended CDs that have 850 MB capacity.

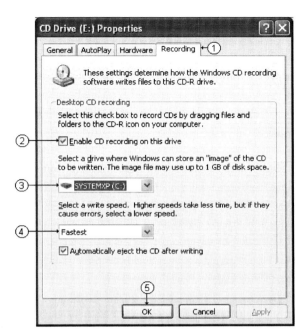

① Click this tab.

② Make sure this option is active.

③ Select the drive where Windows can store an "image" (or temporary file) of the CD you want to write. The size of this file can vary. If you insert a 650 MB CD, Windows automatically reserves up to 700 MB on your hard disk; if you use a 850 MB CD, up to 1 gigabyte will be set aside.

④ Select the speed at which the device will write (this can vary).

⑤ Click to confirm the settings.

Selecting the folders or files you want to copy

▦ **start - My Computer**

▦ To copy a set of files contained in a folder, double-click the folder to open it then select the file(s) concerned.
To copy an entire folder, click its name to select it.

▦ If the files are contained in **My Pictures** or **My Videos**, click either the **Copy to CD** link (if you selected one or more files) or the **Copy all items to CD** link (if you did not select any files, in which case Windows will copy the entire contents of the folder). Windows will then automatically copy the files to its temporary file, ready to be written to your CD.

- If the files are contained in **My Music**, click either the **Copy to audio CD** link (if you selected one or more files or folders) or the **Copy all items to audio CD** (if you did not select any file, in which case Windows will copy the entire contents of the folder).
- In all other cases, when you have selected the file(s) or folder(s), click the **Copy this folder** or **Copy this file** (if you selected only one item) or **Copy all the items** link (if you selected several items). The **Copy Items** dialog box opens: click the name of your CD writer then click the **Copy** button.

Writing the files to the CD-ROM

- **start - My Computer**
- Double-click the CD writer's name.

The list of **Files Ready to Be Written to the CD** *appears.*

- Check and/or modify the list of **Files Ready to Be Written to the CD**.

  It is advisable to go into **Details** *view (*View - Details*) to check that the volume of the file you are copying does not exceed the CD's capacity (cf. 2.2 - E - Preparing the CD writer and your computer).*

- To remove one of the temporary files from the list, click it and press **Del** then confirm with **Yes** (or click the **Delete this file** link in the left pane).
- Start writing to the CD-ROM by clicking the **Write these files to CD** link.
- In the wizard's first dialog box, change the **CD name**, if you wish. By default, Windows gives the current date as the name.
- Click **Next**.

  The CD writing software prepares and writes the files to the CD. When all the files have been copied, the wizard displays a message.

- Click the **Finish** button.

⇨ *If you are copying to a CD-RW (rewritable CD) and that CD contains a file with the same name as one of the files you are writing onto it, the file on the CD will be overwritten by the one you are copying.*

F-Moving folders or files

First method

- In the Explorer, select the folders or files you want to move.
- Click the **Move this folder** or **Move this file** link (according to the object concerned) in the **File and Folder Tasks** frame.
- In the **Move Items** dialog box, expand the hierarchy, if necessary and click the name of the destination folder, then click the **Move** button.

Second method

- Select the folders or the files you want to move.
- Transfer these objects to the clipboard with the **Edit - Cut** command or Ctrl **X**.
- Select the destination folder.
- Paste the contents of the clipboard with **Edit - Paste** or Ctrl **V**.

⇨ *If you make a mistake, you can cancel the move with the Edit - Undo Move command or* Ctrl *Z*.

Third method

- Display the **Folders** bar and select the files concerned.
- Drag them to their destination. If this is on another drive, hold ⇧ Shift down as you drag.

  While you are pointing at the destination folder, the mouse pointer should not have a + sign by it.

  When the transfer is over, the files are no longer visible in the active folder.

G-Renaming a file or folder

- Select the file or folder you want to rename.
- Click the **Rename this file** or **Rename this folder** link (depending on what you selected) in the **File and Folder Tasks** frame.
- Use the normal technique for editing text to change the name of the file or folder and confirm by pressing Enter .

  The name changes automatically. If a file in the same folder already has that name, Windows will refuse your modifications.

H-Deleting folders or files

- Select the files or folders you wish to delete.
- Click the **Delete this file** or **Delete this folder** link (depending on what you selected) in the **File and Folder Tasks** frame or simply press the Del key.
- Click **Yes** to confirm deleting the files and send them to the Recycle Bin.

⇨ *Of course, deleting a folder involves deleting all the files it contains, including any subfolders and all their files.*

⇨ *The deletion is not final: the files still have a physical existence on the disk, but are no longer visible in a folder.*
*To delete the files for good, making space on the disk, remove them from the **Recycle Bin**, or empty this bin.*

⇨ *Be careful: if you delete from a drive other than your own workstation's disk (from a floppy disk or a drive on the network), the deletion is final immediately and you have no way of cancelling it later.*

⇨ *If you would rather not have to confirm each instruction to delete, you can deactivate the **Display delete confirmation dialog** option under the **Global** tab of the **Recycle Bin Properties** dialog box (right-click the **Recycle Bin** in the Folders bar or on the Desktop and choose **Properties**).*

⇨ *To delete files from several different folders, use a search to find them then select them in the **Search Results** window and delete them.*

⇨ *To delete a file from the disk permanently, without using the Recycle Bin, press* ⬚Shift ⬚Del *instead of just* ⬚Del .

I- Managing the files in the Recycle Bin

▦ To view the Recycle Bin's files, double-click the **Recycle Bin** icon on the desktop or open it from the Explorer window (you may need to click the **Folders** button to close the **Folders** bar).

— deletes the bin's contents

— puts all the bin's files back in their original place

*You can see the list of files in the **Recycle Bin**. You can work with this list as with the files in the Explorer window. Its presentation is defined by the options in the **View** menu and the* ⬚⬚▾ *button.*

▦ To retrieve one or more files, select it (them) then click the **Restore this item** or **Restore the selected items** link accordingly.

*You can also right-click the selection and choose the **Restore** option. The files disappear from the Recycle Bin and are once again accessible in the **Explorer** window. If the folder which used to contain the document has been deleted, Windows recreates it.*

To empty the Recycle Bin, right-click its icon and choose **Empty Recycle Bin** or if its window is open, use the **File - Empty Recycle Bin** command or click the **Empty the Recycle Bin** link. Click **Yes** to confirm deleting the files permanently.

⇨ *The Recycle Bin icon on the desktop changes according to its contents: an empty bin is like this:* ⬭ *, a bin with files in it is like this:* ⬭ *.*

J- Compressing files

Compressing in NTFS

This feature is available only to users whose drive (hard disk, partition etc.) is in NTFS format.

start - My Computer

To select a particular file or folder, double-click your personal folder in the **Files Stored on This Computer** list and click the file or folder you want to compress.

Right-click the file or folder you want to compress and click the **Properties** option.

Click the **Advanced** button in the **Attributes** frame on the **General** page.
*If there is no **Advanced** button, this means that your drive is not in NTFS format.*

Tick the **Compress contents to save disk space** option.

Click **OK** on the **Advanced Attributes** dialog box then **OK** on the **Properties** dialog box.

When you compress a folder, Windows will ask you if you wish to compress just the folder or the folder and all its subfolders and files.

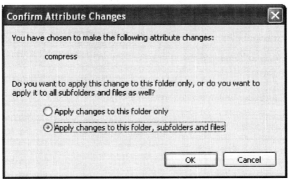

In this case, activate the option of your choice and click **OK**.

⇨ *You cannot encrypt a file compressed with NTFS compression (cf. Protecting your personal folders).*

⇨ *Files or folders compressed in this way appear in colour (blue by default) in the Windows Explorer or My Computer, providing the* **Show encrypted or compressed NTFS files in color** *option is active in* **My Computer - Tools - Folder Options - View** *tab.*

⇨ *To decompress a folder and/or file, deactivate the* **Compress contents to save disk space** *option in the* **Advanced Attributes** *dialog box.*

Compressing into a compressed (zipped) folder

This technique creates a specially compressed folder in which the files/folders you want to zip will be stored.

▓ **start - My Computer**

▓ If necessary, open the folder in which you want to create a compressed folder, but do not select anything.

▓ To create a new compressed folder, open the **File** menu and choose the **New - Compressed (zipped) Folder** option.

If a different compression program has been installed on Windows, the **Compressed (zipped) Folder** *option no longer appears and is replaced by the icon of the new compression program.*

▓ If necessary, change the default name that Window provides then confirm your new name by pressing the ⌨Enter key.

▓ To compress a file or folder, move or copy the required item into the compressed folder using the standard copy and paste techniques (cf. 2.2 - D & F).

⇨ *To send a compressed file as an e-mail attachment, you must send the compressed folder that contains the file.*

⇨ *You can create a compressed folder and compress a file or folder simultaneously. To do this, go to the Windows Explorer or My Computer and right-click the name of the file/folder concerned. Choose the* **Send To - Compressed (zipped) Folder** *option. The file or folder is instantly inserted into a compressed folder, carrying the name of the file or folder you compressed and a .zip extension.*

⇨ *Zipped files and folders remain zipped for both FAT and NTFS drives. They can be moved onto any drive or into any folder on your computer, on the Internet or an intranet. These files are compatible with other file compression ("zip") applications.*

Decompressing a compressed folder

▓ Double-click the name of the compressed folder concerned then click the **Extract all files** link under **Folder Tasks** in the left pane of the window.

▓ Click the **Next** button on the wizard.

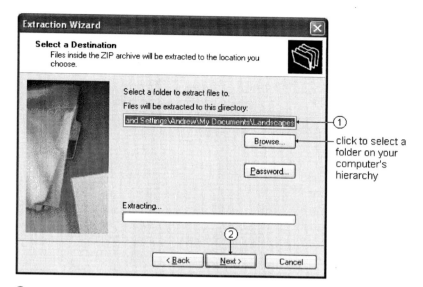

Extraction Wizard

Select a Destination
Files inside the ZIP archive will be extracted to the location you choose.

Select a folder to extract files to.

Files will be extracted to this directory:

`and Settings\Andrew\My Documents\Landscapes` ← ①

[Browse...] ← click to select a folder on your computer's hierarchy

[Password...]

Extracting...

②

[< Back] [Next >] [Cancel]

① Enter the address of the folder in which you want to insert the decompressed files.

② Click this button.

▨ To view the extracted files, activate the **Show extracted files** option.

▨ Click the **Finish** button.

K-Printing a file from inside the Explorer

▨ Select the file(s) concerned.

▨ Right-click the selection, and choose **Print**.

*Depending on the type of file concerned, the information is sent to the Print Manager or if it is an image file, the **Photo Printing Wizard** opens.*

⇨ *You can also activate the **File - Print** command. If the printer icon is present on the desktop, you can also drag the selection onto that icon.*

⇨ *To print the file list, make a screen capture of the required folder ([Prt Sc]) then in the Paint application, paste it in with [Ctrl] V and print this capture from Paint.*

L-Protecting/unprotecting a file

▨ Select the file concerned.

▨ **File - Properties** or [Alt] [Enter]

*You can also right-click the file, then choose **Properties**.*

▨ In the lower part of the dialog box, activate or deactivate the **Read-only** option, to protect or unprotect the selected file.

⇨ *The file is available only for display; it can no longer be modified or deleted without confirmation.*

M-Sending files by electronic mail

▩ Select the files and/or folders concerned.

▩ Right-click to show the selection's shortcut menu.

▩ Point to the **Send To** option and click the **Mail Recipient** option.

Windows starts your e-mail application.

▩ Enter the name(s) of your mail recipient(s) and the subject of your message.

▩ Send the message.

⇨ *The selected files will be sent as attached files.*

N-Opening an application from inside the Explorer

With a program file or a file created by the application

▩ Double-click the icon of the program file or of a file created by the application you wish to open.

⇨ *You can also select a file and press* [Enter] *, or activate the **Open** option in the **File** menu.*

With any data file

It is possible to start an application with any file created by it, or any file with a suitable format.

▩ Double-click the file name, or select it, right-click it then choose **Open With**.

▩ If Windows supplies it, click the name of the program you wish to use or click the **Choose Program** option.

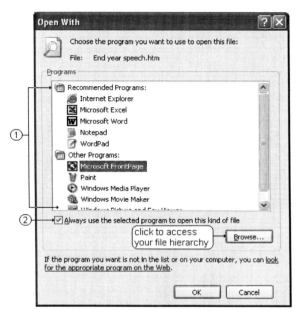

① Select a program to open the file.

② If you want to create an association between this kind of document and the program, activate this option.

2.3 Search Companion

A- Using the Search Companion

▓ To show the **Search** explorer bar, click the **start** button on the taskbar then click the **Search** option or if you are in the Windows Explorer, use the **View - Explorer Bar - Search** command or [🔍 Search] or ⌨ Ctrl **E**.

By default, a little dog called Rover animates the Search Companion pane.

▓ To change the search preferences, click the **Change preferences** link.

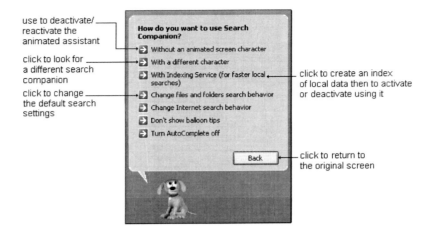

use to deactivate/ reactivate the animated assistant

click to look for a different search companion

click to change the default search settings

How do you want to use Search Companion?

- Without an animated screen character
- With a different character
- With Indexing Service (for faster local searches)
- Change files and folders search behavior
- Change Internet search behavior
- Don't show balloon tips
- Turn AutoComplete off

Back

click to create an index of local data then to activate or deactivate using it

click to return to the original screen

B-Searching on your computer or an intranet

▧ Display the **Search** explorer bar.

What do you want to search for?

- Pictures, music, or video (a)
- Documents (word processing, (b) spreadsheet, etc.)
- All files and folders (c)
- Computers or people (d)
- Information in Help and Support Center

You may also want to...

- Search the Internet
- Change preferences

▧ Depending on what you wish to find, click one of these links:

(a) to look for a multimedia file by its name, or part of its name.

(b) to look for a document using its name (or part thereof) or by its last modification date if necessary.

(c) to search using the name of a file or folder (or a partial name), text within the file/folder and/or using its last modification date, size and so on.

(d) to look for a computer on a network or for one of the people listed in your address book.

According to the link you choose, the Search Companion screen may vary, offering you different options appropriate to the chosen type of search.

As the search method does not differ no matter which link you choose, this chapter describes only how to search for image, music or video files.

*Click the **Pictures, music or video** link:*

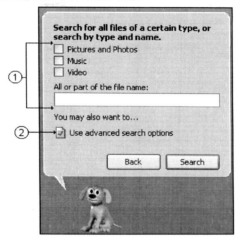

① Click the option(s) corresponding to the type of file you require and/or click the text box and give all or part of the file name that you want to find.

② Click to go to a list of extra criteria (date, size, location etc.).

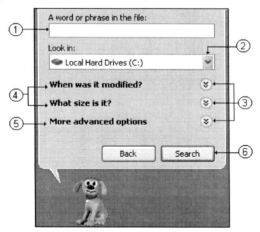

① To look for a word or phrase in the file, click this text box and fill in the text you wish to find.

② Open the list box and click the folder or drive in which the search should be carried out.

③ Click this arrow to see all the criteria available in each category.

④ To include the date on which the file was last modified, or its size, activate the required criteria.

⑤ To search in system files or folders or in hidden files or if you want Windows to differentiate between upper and lower case letters, tick the required options.

⑥ Click to start the search.

*To interrupt the search, click the **Stop** button.*

When the search is over, Windows displays the items it has found:

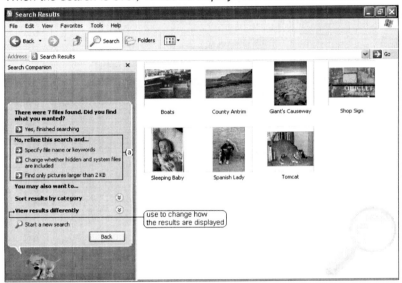

▤ If the search results do not correspond to your needs, you can refine your search with extra criteria (a).

▤ To start a new search using different criteria, use the **Start a new search** link (scroll through the explorer bar, if necessary).

▤ If the search results contain the item you were looking for, click the **Yes, finished searching** link to close the Search Companion pane and keep the found files in the pane on the right.

C-Searching on the Internet

▓ Display the **Search** explorer bar and make sure your Internet connection is open.

▓ Click the **Search the Internet** link.

*If you do not see this link, click the **Change preferences** link then click **Change files and folders search behavior**. Activate the **Standard** option and click **OK**.*

*If the **Search** bar still remains blank, click the **Customize** button at the top of it. Click the **Reset** button then **OK**. After a brief wait, you should obtain the Internet search bar.*

▓ To activate or deactivate certain search engines, click the **Customize** button.

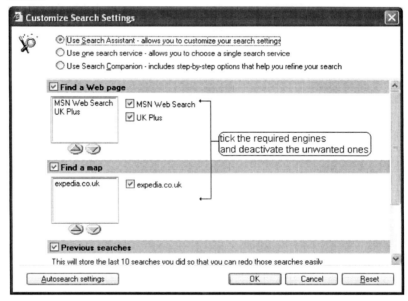

Searching for a Web page

▦ In the Internet **Search** bar, click one of the search categories, depending on your needs:

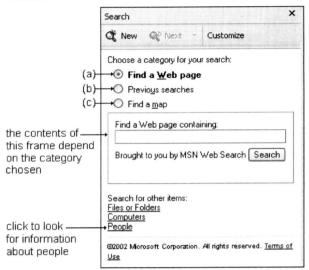

(a)   to search the Net using the keyword(s) you enter in the **Find a Web page containing** box.

(b)   you can reuse one of the last ten searches made, as these are saved automatically providing the **Previous searches** option has been ticked (**Customize** button). If this is the case, the last ten searches are listed as hyperlinks in the **You've run the following searches** box.

(c)   to look for an address, place or region using the Expedia.com (or Expedia.co.uk) search engine. You can find maps of the UK, USA, France and Germany and links concerning other locations.

2.4 Drives

A·Formatting a floppy disk

▦ From the **My Computer** or **Windows Explorer** window, right-click the icon of your floppy disk drive.

▦ Click the **Format** option.

① Define the capacity of the floppy disk according to its physical characteristics: for a High Density floppy disk, choose **1.44MB**, for a Low
Density floppy disk, choose **720KB**.

② If necessary, indicate the type of file system and the allocation unit
size to apply to the disk.

③ If required, specify the name you want to give your floppy disk.

④ If your floppy disk has already been formatted, activate this option;
Windows deletes the contents of the floppy disk, without checking the
sectors on the disk.

⑤ Click to start formatting.

▓ Click the **OK** button to confirm that you want to format your floppy disk.

⇨ *To **Create an MS-DOS startup disk** to boot the system from an MS-DOS
prompt, tick the appropriate option before formatting the disk. This floppy
disk will not contain any other tools.*

B-Changing the label of a drive

▓ Right-click the drive icon (in the Windows Explorer or the My Computer
window) and click the **Properties** option.

▓ Under the **General** tab, give the new name for the drive (1 to 11 characters) in the text box.

▓ Click **OK**.

⇨ *You can also change the label of a drive by right-clicking the drive concerned and choosing the **Rename** option.*

C-Viewing your system's properties

▧ Click the **start** button and go to the **Control Panel**. Click **Performance and Maintenance** then click the **System** link.

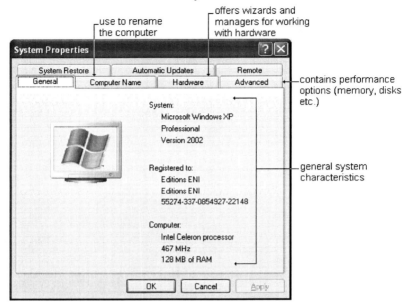

use to rename the computer

offers wizards and managers for working with hardware

contains performance options (memory, disks etc.)

general system characteristics

3.1 Windows Movie Maker

A-Looking at the Movie Maker window

▒ **start** - **All Programs** - **Accessories** - **Windows Movie Maker**

The **collections area** (a), where you can arrange the sound, video or still picture files that you create or import. A list of your collections appears in the pane on the left (b) and the clips belonging to the current collection are listed in the middle pane (c).

The **monitor** (d), where you can view a particular clip or an entire project. It contains a **seek bar** (e) which changes position when you play a sound or video file or view a still picture. There is also a set of buttons (f) for moving around in the clip or project (**Play, Pause, Stop, Full Screen,** etc.).

The **workspace** (g), where you create and edit your projects before saving them as a video sequence. By clicking the appropriate option in the **View** menu, you can display this area in **Storyboard** view or in **Timeline** view. When the **Timeline** is active, two bars appear in the workspace: the first is where the video clips and fixed pictures are displayed and the second (the **audio bar**) is for sound clips.

B-Recording source material

Before you show your movie, you must save sound and/or video material in Windows Movie Maker, by converting it to Windows Media digital format. Once this is done, the source material appears as clips which can be included in a project, or in several projects. You can record source material with a capture device such as a digital (or analogue) video camera, a Webcam or a microphone.

Recording from an analogue cassette

▓ **File**
    Record

Ctrl R

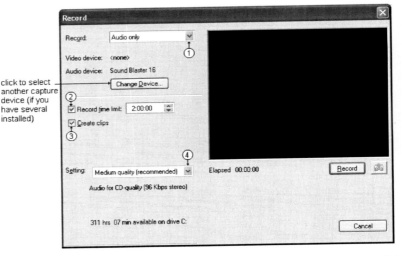

① Open this list and click the option corresponding to the type of material you want to record.

② If you want to record for a set time then stop automatically, make sure that this check box is ticked then either type the time into the text box or use the increment buttons.

③ Tick the check box if you want Movie Maker to split up the sequence into clips.

④ Choose the quality you want to use for your recording.

▓ Use the commands on your video recorder or your analogue video camera to locate the source material you want to record.

▓ Click the **Record** button.

The word Recording flashes to let you know that recording is in progress.

▓ Use the controls of your video recorder or analogue video camera to play the source material you want to record: you can see the video materiel on the preview screen.

- If you chose to record for a set time, recording will stop automatically once the time limit has been reached; to interrupt the recording manually, click the **Stop** button.

- Select the drive and the folder in which the file should be recorded then enter the **File name** in the corresponding text box and click **Save**.

  A new collection containing the material you have recorded appears in the collection area's left pane. The clips created from the material appear in the right pane.

- Use the controls of your video recorder or your analogue video camera to stop the cassette.

Recording material with a digital video device connected to an IEEE 1394 card (FireWire)

This feature is available provided that your computer has a processor speed of at least 600 MHz and is equipped with an IEEE 1394 card.

- Check that your video camera or your digital video recorder is properly connected, with the recorded video installed then set your device to read mode.

- **File**   **R**
  Record

  *Movie Maker may display the **Record** dialog box as soon as you connect your video device: in this case you do not need to select the **File - Record** command.*

- Use the controls on your digital video device to position the tape just before the place where you want to start recording.

- Start playing and click the **Record** button.

  *The word **Recording** flashes in the dialog box to let you know that recording is in progress and the **Record** button changes into a **Stop** button.*

- Click the **Stop** button when you want to stop recording.

- In the **Save Windows Media File** window, select the drive or folder where you want to store the new file then specify its name in the **File name** box.

  Windows will save the file in .wmv format.

- Click the **Save** button.

  *The video appears as a sequence of clips, provided you activated the **Create clips** option in the **Record** dialog box.*

- To view the clips, use the buttons under the preview frame in the right-hand pane.

Recording a narration

- Activate the **Timeline** view of the workspace, if you need to, by using the **View - Timeline** command or by clicking the ⬛ button in the workspace.

Use **File - Open Project** or ⌃ **O** to open the project to which you want to add a narration.

File - Record Narration or click 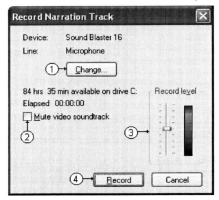 in the workspace

Record Narration Track

Device: Sound Blaster 16
Line: Microphone

①→[Change...]

84 hrs 35 min available on drive C: Record level
Elapsed 00:00:00
☐ Mute video soundtrack
②

③→

④→[Record]   [Cancel]

① If the capture device or the line that appears at the top of the dialog box is not the right one, click this button and modify the settings.
If you want to use a microphone, choose the **Mic Volume** option from the **Input line** list.

② If your project contains a video clip that includes sound and you do not want to hear this soundtrack, activate this option.

③ Increase or decrease the volume of your narration.

④ Click to record the narration.

As you record your narration, the project runs in the monitor.

When you have finished, click the **Stop** button.

In the **Save in** list, select the drive and the folder where you want to store the sound file then specify its name in the **File name** box and click **Save**.

The narration is saved as a .wav sound file. It is automatically inserted as a sound clip at the beginning of the project's audio bar. You can see this bar in the workspace and in the current collection:

If you need to, you can move the sound clip underneath the video clips and/or still pictures to which the commentary refers.

C-Importing a file

You can import various files into Windows Movie Maker:

- ***video files***: *.wmv, .asf, .avi*
- ***video clip (MPEG) files***: *.mpeg, .mpg, .mlv, .mp2, .mpa, .mpe*
- ***audio files***: *.mp3, .wav, .snd, .au, .aif, .aifc, .aiff, .wma*

- *Windows Media files*: .afs, .wm, .wma, .wmv
- *still pictures*: .jpg, .jpeg, .jpe, .jfif, .gif, .dib.

As with a source video sequence that you have just recorded, an imported file appears as a series of clips, which you can include in one or more projects.

▨ Click the collection into which you want to import the file.

▨ **File - Import** or ⌈Ctrl⌋ I

▨ In the **Look in** list, select the drive and the folder where the file is located.

▨ Select the file you want to import: to import several files, ⌈⇧ Shift⌋-click to select them if they appear consecutively in the list or ⌈Ctrl⌋-click to select them if not.

▨ Click the **Open** button to import the file(s).

*If you import a sound file or a still image file, the new clips are inserted into the current collection. If you import a video file, Windows Movie Maker puts the clips in a new collection, located in the **My Collections** folder. By default, this collection takes the name of the original imported file.*

⇨ *The source files used in Windows Movie Maker remain in their original locations. The clips in the collections area do not physically exist there, but appear by means of a formula that creates a link to the source file. If you try to work with clips whose source file has been deleted, moved or renamed, Windows Movie Maker prompts you to search for it. Click the **Yes** button only if the source file has been moved: the **Find** dialog box cannot be used to retrieve a deleted file or to identify one that has been renamed.*

⇨ *To specify a default file import path, use **View - Options**, then in the **Import path** text box, give the required address or use the **Browse** button to select it.*

D-Creating title slides with Microsoft Paint

▨ Open the **Microsoft Paint** application (**start** button - **All Programs - Accessories - Paint**).

▨ **Image - Attributes** or ⌈Ctrl⌋ E

▨ Type **320** in the **Width** box and **240** in the **Height** box.

▨ Activate the **Pixels** option in the **Units** frame.

▨ Click **OK**.

▨ Create the picture (text and/or illustration).

▨ Use **File - Save** or ⌈Ctrl⌋ **S**, then select the drive then the folder where you want to store the picture file.

▨ Give the **File name** then click the **Save** button.

▨ Go back into the Windows Movie Maker window, import the picture you have created (cf. 3.1 - C - Importing a file) then add it to the project concerned.

E- Changing the properties of a clip

▓ Click the collection containing the clip in question then click the clip itself.

▓ **View - Properties** or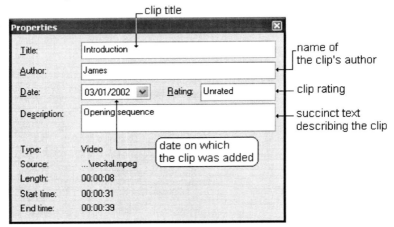

▓ If necessary, change the **Title** of the clip, its **Author**, its creation **Date** and a **Description** of the clip by filling in the appropriate text boxes.

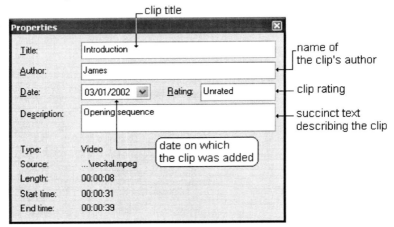

▭clip title

Properties	⊠
Title:	Introduction
Author:	James
Date:	03/01/2002 ⌄ Rating: Unrated
Description:	Opening sequence
Type:	Video
Source:	...\recital.mpeg
Length:	00:00:08
Start time:	00:00:31
End time:	00:00:39

⌐name of
└the clip's author

── clip rating

── succinct text
describing the clip

(date on which
the clip was added)

⇨ *You can change only the properties of clips which appear in the collec-*
tions area. You cannot change the properties of those displayed in the
workspace. If you add a clip to the workspace and then change its proper-
ties in the collections area, the clip in the workspace will keep its old
properties.

F- Creating a collection

▓ In the left pane of the collections area, click the name of the collection in which you want to create the new collection.

*You can also select a collection by opening the **Collection** drop-down list on the **Location** toolbar then clicking the name of the collection you want to select.*

▓ **File - New - Collection** or

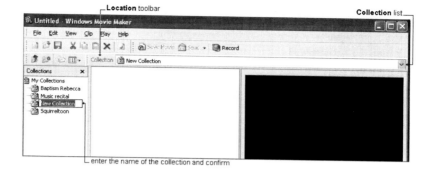

enter the name of the collection and confirm

G-Managing clips/collections

▓ To change the view of the clips list, select one of the following options from the **View** menu:

Thumbnails   displays each clip as a bitmap image with a title.

List   displays a list of the names of all the clips.

Details   displays a list containing the names and properties of all the clips.

The view you select is applied to the clips in all the collections (the same options can be found by opening the list on the ⊞▾ tool button on the Collections toolbar).

▓ To move a selected collection, drag the selected collection name into its new position.

▓ To copy or move clips, select the clips and drag them into the new position, holding down the Ctrl key as you drag if you wish to make a copy.

▓ To rename a clip or collection, select the collection or clip concerned and either click the name again or use the **Edit - Rename** command. Type the new name and press Enter .

⇨ *You can also rename a clip or collection by right-clicking its name then choosing the* **Rename** *option. You can also use a right-click to* **Delete** *a clip or collection.*
You can rename only the clips that appear in the collections area; you cannot rename the ones displayed in the workspace. If you add a clip to the workspace and then rename it in the collections area, the clip in the workspace will keep its old name.

▓ To delete a selected clip or collection, use **Edit - Delete** or ☒ or Del then click **Yes** to confirm the deletion.

H-Opening a project

A project is made up of clips, which you can see in the workspace. You can save your project as a movie in a video file.

▓ **File** 　　　　 Ctrl **O**
Open Project

▓ Using the **Look in** list, select the drive and the folder where the project is located.

▓ Select the project you want to open, in the main part of the dialog box.

▓ Click the **Open** button.

The project appears in the workspace.

⇨ *To create a new project, use the* **File** *-* **New** *-* **Project** *command or* Ctrl *N or click the* ⬚ *tool button on the* **Standard** *toolbar.*

I- Saving a new project

▓ **File** 　　　　 Ctrl **S**
Save Project

▓ Select the drive and the folder where you want to store the project, then enter a name for the project in the **File name** box.

▓ Click the **Save** button.

⇨ *Windows Movie Maker project files have the extension MSWMM.*

J- Adding a clip to a project

▤ ▓ Display the **Timeline** view (**View - Timeline** or click ⬚).

This action is necessary if you want to work with audio files.

▓ Click the name of the collection that contains the clip you want to add to the project then select the clip(s) concerned.

▓ **Clip - Add To Storyboard/Timeline**

⇨ *Video clips and still pictures are displayed in the first bar in the workspace. Sound clips appear on the second bar, known as the* **audio bar**, *when you are in* **Timeline** *view.*

🖱 ▓ Display the **Timeline** view (**View - Timeline** or click ⬚).

This action is necessary if you want to work with audio files.

▓ Click the name of the collection that contains the clip you want to add to the project then select the clip(s) concerned.

▓ Point to the selected clip(s) and drag it/them into the workspace. Drag video clips or still pictures onto the first bar and drag sound clips onto the second bar (audio bar).

Release the mouse button when the blue vertical bar reaches the position in the project where you want to insert the clips (in front of the first clip, after the last or between two clips).

K-Trimming a clip

If you want to use only part of a clip in your project, you can trim away the rest. You can remove material from the beginning and/or the end of a clip. This operation has no effect on the source material, which remains intact.

If necessary, display the **Timeline** view (**View - Timeline**).

In the workspace, click the clip you want to trim.

The clip appears on the monitor.

To trim away the beginning of the clip, point to the slider on the monitor's seek bar (⬛), drag it to the end of the section you want to remove, then use the command **Clip - Set Start Trim Point** (or Ctrl ⇧ Shift ←): the material is trimmed off from the beginning of the clip up to the position of the cursor.

To trim away the end of the clip, point to the slider on the preview screen's seek bar, drag it to the beginning of the section you want to remove then use the command **Clip - Set End Trim Point** (or Ctrl ⇧ Shift →): the material from the position of the cursor to the end of the clip is trimmed off.

You can trim the beginning of a clip, the end of a clip or both.

In the workspace, click the clip you wish to trim.

The clip appears in the monitor.

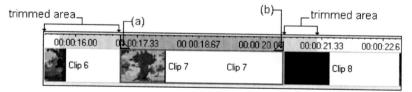

To trim away the beginning of the clip, point to the start trim marker (a) in the workspace and drag it to the end of the section you want to remove.

To trim away the end of the clip, point to the end trim marker (b) and drag it to the beginning of the section you want to remove.

As you drag the trim markers, the clip plays on the monitor so that you can find the exact point at which to make the cut.

⇨ *If you change your mind about trimming a clip, you can cancel all the trim points set: select the clip and use* **Clip - Clear Trim Points** *(or* Ctrl ⇧ Shift Del *).*

L-Splitting a clip

You may want to split a video or sound clip (for example) in two so that you can insert another clip (video, sound or still picture) in the middle of it, or so that you can create a transition. You can split a clip in the workspace or work directly with a clip in the collections area.

▓ In the workspace or in the collections area, select the clip that you want to split.

▓ Point to the slider on the seek bar and drag it to the position where you want to split the clip.

▓ **Clip**      (on the monitor   [Ctrl] [⇧ Shift] **S**
    Split   bar)

The first clip keeps its original name, while the second clip uses the same name followed by a number. In this example, clip 3 has been split, generating clip 3(1):

⇨ *If you split a clip in the workspace, the clip in the collections area remains intact and vice-versa.*

⇨ *You can also combine two or more clips to create a single clip. Select them in the workspace or the collections area (use [Ctrl]-clicks) and use* **Clip - Combine** *or* [Ctrl] [⇧ Shift] **C**. *The new clip adopts the name and properties of the first clip in the group you combined.*

M-Applying transitions

When a transition is applied between two clips, the frames of the first clip disappear gradually while the frames of the second clip appear.

▓ Display the workspace in **Timeline** view.

▓ In the workspace, select the second of the two clips between which you want to create a transition then drag towards the left so that the second clip overlaps the first clip.

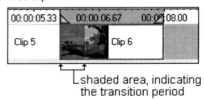

└ shaded area, indicating
the transition period

⇨ *To change the length of the transition, make sure that the two clips involved are displayed in the workspace and select the second (the overlapping clip on the right). Drag it towards the left to make the transition longer or towards the right to make it shorter.*

⇨ To remove a transition, drag the overlapping clip on the right further to the right, so that it no longer overlaps the clip to its left.

⇨ To adjust the audio level, use the **Edit - Audio Levels** command or click 🔲 on the workspace. To increase the sound level of the audio track, drag the slider to the right; to increase the level of the video track, drag the slider to the left.

N-Previewing a clip/project

▓ Select the collection or open the project containing the clip(s) you want to view.

▓ To preview a clip, or a set of clips, select them in the collections area or, if they have been added to a project, select them in the workspace then use the **Play - Play/Pause** command or ⬤ or [space].

▓ To preview all the clips in a project, use **Play - Play Entire Storyboard/ Timeline**.

▓ To stop the preview, use **Play - Stop** or click ⬤.

The monitor automatically displays the first clip in the project visible in the workspace. If no project is open, the monitor contains nothing.

▓ To pause the preview, use **Play - Play/Pause** or click ⬤ (the simplest way to start the preview again is to click ⬤).

▓ To display the preview full-screen, open the **Play** menu and choose either **Play/Pause** or **Play Entire Storyboard/Timeline** then use **Play - Full Screen** or [Alt][Enter] or ⬤. To close the full screen window, click in it.

⇨ You can use the ⬤ and ⬤ buttons to display the **Previous Frame** and **Next Frame** of the clip in the monitor and the ⬤ and ⬤ buttons to show the last screen **Back** and the **Next** screen of the project.

O-Saving a movie in a file

When your project is complete, you can save it as a movie, which you can view on your computer, attach to an e-mail, transfer to a Web server or copy onto a CD-ROM.

▓ Create or open the project you want to save as a movie.

▓ **File - Save Movie** or [Ctrl] **M**
You can also use the Save Movie tool button 🔲.

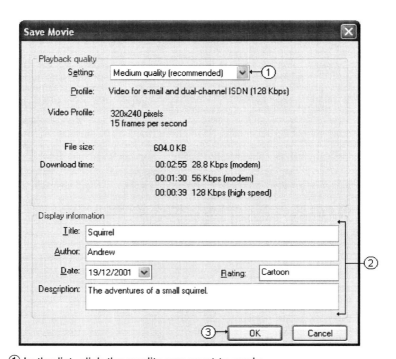

① In the list, click the quality you want to apply.

If your movie is to be viewed on a colour portable device, open the **Setting** list and click **Other**. Open the **Profile** list and choose the **Video for color PDA devices (225 Kbps)** or **Video for color PDA devices (150 Kbps)** option. These profiles are optimised for viewing with portable devices that can read Windows Media format.

If your movie is to be saved onto a Web server, open the **Setting** list and click **Other**. Open the **Profile** list and choose the **Video for Web servers (28.8 Kbps)** or **Video for Web servers (56 Kbps)** option, depending on the type of server being used.

② Fill in the information that Movie Maker should display when the movie plays.

③ Click to confirm.

▓ Select the drive and the folder in which you want to store the movie.

▓ To save a movie, you can:

- save onto your hard disk: select the **My Videos** folder within the **My Documents** folder.

- save into a Web folder: click **My Network Places** and select the Web folder in which you wish to save the movie (of course, to do this, you must have the appropriate permissions).

- write it onto a CD-ROM: select the drive that corresponds to your CD writer, making sure it contains a blank CD-R or CD-RW.

▓ Give a name for the movie in the **File name** box and click the **Save** button.

A message then informs you that the movie has been saved and asks if you would like to play it now.

▓ Click **Yes** to play the movie in Windows Media Player or **No** to return to the Windows Movie Maker window.

▓ If you choose to watch the movie, the Windows Media Player opens. To play the movie, click the ⊙ button. When you have finished playing the movie, click the ▓ or ▓ button to close the Windows Media Player window.

▓ If you chose to save your movie on a CD-ROM, follow the usual procedure (cf. 2.2 - E - Copying a file or folder onto a CD-ROM).

⇨ *A movie file has a .WMV name extension.*

⇨ *You can use the File - Send Movie To - E-mail command to send a movie to one or more e-mail recipients. To play the movie in Windows Media Player, the recipient(s) must open the message then double-click the movie file icon to start the Media Player.*

P-Transferring a movie to a Web server

You can transfer a movie onto a Web server so that it can be accessed from the Internet or an intranet. After sending the movie to the Web server, you should create a Web page and insert an hyperlink into it so that network users who open your Web page can view your movie by clicking the link.

▓ Create or open the project that you want to put on the Web server.

▓ **File - Send Movie To - Web Server**

▓ Open the **Setting** list and click the quality you want to use.

▓ Open the **Profile** list and choose a different profile, if you wish.

▓ Use the text boxes in the **Display information** frame to fill in the information to display when the file plays then click **OK**.

▓ Enter a file name for your movie in the text box provided in the **Name the movie to send** dialog box then click the **OK** button.

The movie is saved as a Windows Media file, with a .wmv extension.

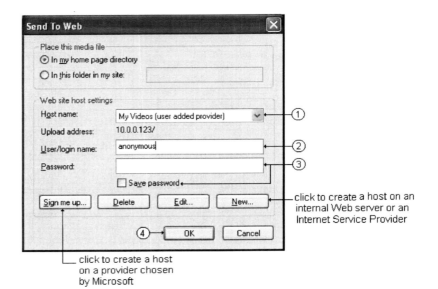

Send To Web

Place this media file
- ⊙ In my home page directory
- ○ In this folder in my site:

Web site host settings

Host name: My Videos (user added provider) ── ①

Upload address: 10.0.0.123/

User/login name: anonymous ── ②

Password: ── ③

☐ Save password

[Sign me up...] [Delete] [Edit...] [New...] ── click to create a host on an internal Web server or an Internet Service Provider

④ ─ [OK] [Cancel]

click to create a host on a provider chosen by Microsoft

① Select a host name (a host profile is the configuration defining the necessary settings for saving movies onto an FTP server and publishing movies on a Web server) then click **OK**.

② Enter your user name, which is often the first part of your e-mail address.

③ Enter the password and if you wish, tick the **Save password** option.

④ Send the movie onto the Web server.

The Sending To Web dialog box shows you how the transfer is progressing. Once the movie has been successfully published on the Web, Windows gives you the opportunity to visit the site.

▨ Click the **View Site Now** button to visit the Web site or close the **Sending To Web** dialog box by clicking its ❌ button.

▨ Create the Web page containing a hyperlink to the movie file which you have just published on the Web.

3.2 Windows Media Player

A-Discovering the Windows Media Player

▓ **start - All Programs - Windows Media Player**

You can also find the Windows Media Player option with start - All Programs - Accessories - Entertainment.

The contents of the main part of this window vary, depending on whether you are playing a CD, a DVD or have your Internet connection open. If you are online, the WindowsMedia.com site will offer you the latest news and information on music, radio, video and so on.

▓ The Windows Media Player window consists of:

(a) **A title bar and menus**: this area appears automatically when you point to the **Playlist Selection** area.

(b) **Playlist Selection** area: you can use the buttons in this area to choose a playlist or another type of element, but also to manage the playlist and certain tools.

(c) **Features Taskbar**: this bar contains seven default buttons which control the main Player features.

(d) **Playback Controls** area: these commands can be used to adjust the volume and control playback for audio and video files.

B-Playing an audio CD

▓ Open the **Windows Media Player** application (**start - All Programs - Windows Media Player**) then insert an audio CD in your CD-ROM drive.

track currently playing

Playlist pane

use to change the visualization

Selecting and playing a track on an audio CD

▓ Click the **Now Playing** button, if necessary.

▓ In the **Playlist** pane, click the required track.

▓ Click the button on the **Playback Controls** area to start playing the track (once you activate it, this button changes into).

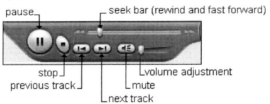

pause

seek bar (rewind and fast forward)

stop
previous track

volume adjustment
mute
next track

The track currently playing appears in green in the Playlist pane and the length already played is shown at the bottom right of the window.

⇨ *The **View - Visualizations** menu (on the menu bar) also offers a choice of visualization effects for the Now Playing page.*

Finding information about a CD

If your Internet connection is open the first time you play a CD, the Windows Media Player will look on the WindowsMedia.com site for information about the CD you are playing (the artist's name, the composer and the track titles) and display this in the Player window. If it finds this information, Windows saves it on your hard disk to make it available the next time you play the CD.

If there is no information available concerning the CD or if your PC is not connected to the Internet, the Windows Media Player will show "Artist Unknown" and display the tracks as a numbered list instead of using their names.

▦ To start an Internet search manually for the name of the artist, the album tracks, the cover art and so on, make sure your Internet connection is online.

▦ Click the **Copy from CD** button, then the **Get Names** ⬤ button.

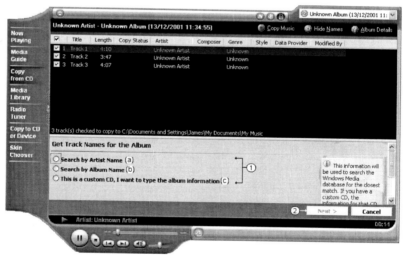

① To **Search by Artist Name** (a) or **Search by Album Name** (b), tick the corresponding option then enter the name you are looking for, in the option's text box (which appears only once you have activated the option).

If you want to enter the CD information yourself (perhaps for one of your 'home-made' CDs), activate option (c).

② Click to go to the next step.

▦ If you are entering the album information yourself, fill in the form provided and click **Next**. Check what you have entered and click **Finish**.

▦ If you chose to search the Internet using the name of the artist or the album, the search now starts.

MULTIMEDIA APPLICATIONS

If the Windows Media Player does not find the information required, you can click the **Search Again** button to try searching again or give more detailed information about the album concerned:

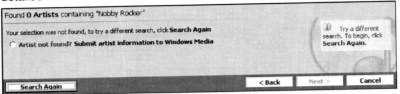

Found 0 Artists containing "Nobby Rocker"

Your selection was not found, to try a different search, click **Search Again**

○ **Artist not found? Submit artist information to Windows Media**

Try a different search. To begin, click Search Again.

Search Again   < Back   Next >   Cancel

In this case, activate the **Artist** (or **Album) not found?** option and click **Next**. Fill in the form, giving any other information you have (the type of music, a track title, etc.), click **Next** then **Finish** to start searching again.

⇨ *To display the album information about a CD in the Media Library, show the Media Library, click the Album category then right-click the album concerned and choose Info (or click the Media Details button directly).*

C-Media Player and DVDs

Playing a DVD

To play a DVD, your computer must have not only a DVD drive installed, but also a DVD decoder program, such as WinDVD (InterVideo Inc.) or PowerDVD (CyberLink Corp).

Before playing a DVD, you should make sure that the screen saver has been turned off. To do this, use **Tools - Options** on the Media Player menu bar, and on the **Player** page, make sure the **Allow screen saver during playback** option is not active.

Insert the DVD in the appropriate drive.

The Windows Media Player can start playing a DVD automatically, but if Windows XP has several DVD applications installed and if the Media Player is not open, you may see this dialog box, in which you can choose what action to take with the DVD:

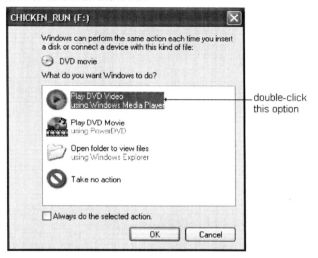

— double-click this option

*The contents of the DVD appear in the **Playlist** pane.*

▓ To view the chapters for a title, click the + sign to the left of the title concerned. To hide the chapters for a title, click the - sign.

▓ To play a DVD manually, use the **Play - DVD or CD Audio** command, or you can open the [📄 My playlist ▼] list and click the name of the DVD you want to play.

▓ In the **Playlist** pane, click the title or chapter of the DVD you want to play.

▓ To view your DVD in full screen mode, select the **View - Full Screen** command or press [Alt][Enter] or click the [🔲] button.

When you switch to full screen view, the Player controls appear briefly before disappearing again:

returns to the Windows Media Player window ⎯
hides/displays the playlist pane ⎯

▓ To restore these controls to the screen, move your mouse or press any key.

MULTIMEDIA APPLICATIONS

⇨ *To specify any **Parental control** or **Language settings**, select **Tools - Options - DVD** tab and choose the required options.*

Activating the Now Playing Tools

▨ **View - Now Playing Tools**

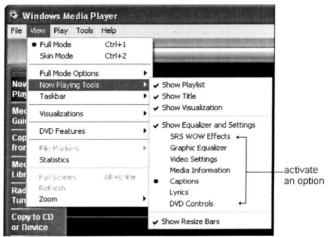

▨ The active tool appears towards the bottom of the screen. To activate another option, click the ▣ button then select the option you want.

*You can also use the **View - Now Playing Tools** command and click the required option.*

▨ To hide the **Equalizer and Settings** tool, use the **View - Now Playing Tools** command and click the **Show Equalizer and Settings** option to deactivate it.

Capturing a still picture from a DVD

▨ Play the DVD concerned.

▨ **View - DVD Features - Image Capture**

*The **Image Capture** command will be available only if your graphics card and your DVD decoder support this feature.*

▨ If necessary, select the folder in which you want to save the image then enter the **File name**.

▨ If necessary, change the **Save as type** option, then click the **Save** button.

D-Managing multimedia files with the Media Library

Looking at the Media Library

▓ Click the **Media Library** button on the Player's taskbar.

the files are organized in categories

contents of the selected category

▓ To show the contents of one of these categories, click the + sign associated with it. Conversely, to hide the contents of a category, click its - sign.

Defining Media Library access rights

▓ **Tools - Options - Media Library** tab

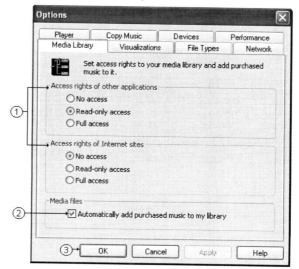

① Tick an option:

No access: to prohibit all access to your library by programs installed on your computer and/or by Internet sites.

Read-only access: to authorize programs and/or Internet sites to read your playlists and your digital multimedia files.

Full access: to authorize programs and/or Internet sites to write in your playlists, enabling them to change your Media Library entries.

② If you want Windows to add licensed music you buy online to the Media Library automatically, tick this option.

③ Click to confirm your choices.

Adding tracks from a CD to the Media Library

▨ Insert a CD into the CD-ROM drive and click **Copy from CD**.

▨ If necessary, deactivate any tracks that you do not want to copy (by default, all the tracks are activated).

You can click the ☑ *box at the top of the list to activate or deactivate all the check boxes.*

▨ Click the **Copy Music** button.

If author copyright protection is activated the first time you use the Copy Music button, a message appears to remind you that you cannot copy protected (or licensed) tracks copied from a CD onto another computer. Click OK or deactivate the Do not protect content check box and click OK.

The selected track(s) are copied into the My Music folder by default and are classified in the Media Library. The My Music folder contains subfolders carrying the name of the artist or the name Various Artists if several different artists feature on the album. You can ask Windows to save your music files in a different folder if you wish.

⇨ *To add a file from a computer or an Internet site, open the File menu then click the Open option (if the file you want to copy is on your computer or a workstation in your network) or the Open URL option (if the file is on an Internet site). Locate and select the file you want to add then follow the file copying procedure described previously.*

⇨ *To add files to the Media Library automatically as you play them, use Tools - Options, activate the Player tab and click the Add item to Media Library when played option.*

⇨ *You can also copy tracks from a CD using the File - Copy - Copy from Audio CD command. Next, click the CD-ROM drive, if several drives are installed on your machine. Select the tracks you want to copy and click Copy Music.*

E-Creating a playlist

You can create a series of tracks in a playlist that you can then use in various ways, such as writing onto a CD.

▓ To create a new list, click **Media Library** then the **New playlist** button. Enter the new playlist name then click **OK**.

The new playlist is included automatically in the My Playlists category in the Media Library.

▓ To add files to the playlist, click the item concerned in the Media Library then click the **Add to playlist** button.

▓ Click the name of the playlist into which you want to add the selected item.

▓ Add as many elements as you wish, although you should keep a check on the total volume of the playlist if you are going to copy it later onto a CD.

Only items from the Media Library can be added to a playlist!

⇨ *To delete a playlist, right-click that playlist's name in the Media Library then click the **Delete** option.*

F- Creating your own CD

You can use the Windows Media Player to copy tracks stored in your Media Library onto a CD. However, you cannot copy live incoming data, such as a radio station transmission.
The Windows Media Player cannot copy tracks onto a CD-RW that has already been used, unless you delete its current contents with another program or using the My Computer commands. You can copy .wma (Windows Media format), .mp3 and .wav files.

Copying files onto an audio CD

▓ Click the **Copy to CD or Device** button or use **File - Copy - Copy to Audio CD**.

The Select music to copy window is divided into two parts, with the Music to Copy list on the left and on the right the Music on Device list.

number of items copied and the total length

① Click this button then choose the playlist or track category that you want to copy.

② If necessary, deactivate the check boxes of any tracks that you do not want to copy, then insert a CD-R or a CD-RW into your CD writer.

③ If you have several writers, click this button then select the CD writer containing the blank CD.

④ Click to start copying.

Before starting to write on the CD, Windows checks the tracks and converts them to the file type that suits the CD.

*Look in the **Status** column in the **Music to Copy** pane to see how the conversion or copying process is progressing:*

⇨ *You should avoid running other actions while you are writing a CD as this can cause the CD writer to stop.*

⇨ *If you have problems with the CD writer, you can check or modify its settings. Use **Tools - Options - Devices** tab, click the device concerned then the **Properties** button. The recording speed settings, among others, can be found under the **Recording** tab.*

Copying files onto a portable device

▦ Click the **Copy to CD or Device** button or use **File - Copy - Copy to Portable Device**.

▦ Click the ⌄ button on the **Music to Copy** pane then choose the playlist or track category that you want to copy from the **Media Library**.

▦ If necessary, deactivate the check boxes of any tracks that you do not want to copy.

▦ Click the ⌄ button in the **Music on Device** pane then select the device to which you wish to copy the files.

▦ Click the **Copy Music** button at the top right of the window.

Windows checks the space available on the device then converts the files and copies them onto the portable device.

⇨ *You should let the Player determine the quality level automatically as it copies audio files, or the copy may take a long time.*

⇨ *If you want to see the portable device's settings for audio file quality levels, click the ⬤ button.*

G-Listening to the radio

▦ Make sure your Internet connection is open.

▦ Click the **Radio Tuner** button.

shows/hides the contents of each category

click to listen
to that station

the station
links are
divided into
three categories

To make a station search, click one of the required radio types (a), or enter in the text box (b) a keyword representing the station you want to find. If you enter a keyword, finish by clicking the button.

WindowsMedia.com lists the stations that correspond to your search and also offers to complement your search request with more criteria:

click to go back to the previous page

use to combine search criteria

valid only in the USA

▨ To find a station using an advanced search, click the **Use Advanced Search** option.

▨ This provides several search options, allowing you to search by several criteria. Fill in these options by opening the attached drop-down list:

Any Genre to choose a particular style of station.

Any Language to choose a specific broadcasting language.

Any Country to choose a specific geographical location.

Any Speed to choose a particular transmission speed.

Any Band to choose an **AM, FM** or **Net Only** station.

▨ You can use the **Keyword** text box to enter a description by which to search, such as "quiz" or "talkback" to find stations which present those types of show.

- Click the ![] button to start the search.
- To add a station to your list of favourite stations, click the link for the radio station to display the details about it, then click the ![] **Add to My Stations** button.
- To see the list of your favourite stations, open the **My Stations** category by clicking the corresponding button ⬦.

⇨ *The references of your favourite stations are also saved in your Media Library in the Radio Tuner Presets category.*

H-Changing the look of the Windows Media Player

① Click this button.

② Click one of the skins offered.

③ To apply the selected skin to the Windows Media Player, click here.

MULTIMEDIA APPLICATIONS

The Windows Media Player takes on the selected appearance. This is always divided into two sections:

click to return
to full mode or
press [Ctrl] 1

▦ To adopt the **Skin Mode** again, take the **Skin Mode** option in the **View** menu or press [Ctrl] **2**.

3.3 Digital Photos

A-Setting up a folder to contain pictures

You can store your photos in the My Pictures folder that Windows XP provides or create other folders for this purpose (cf. 2.2 - C - Creating a folder).

▦ If you are saving images in a folder other than **My Pictures**, make sure that your folder is either the **Pictures** type or the **Photo Album** type, so that Windows XP will associate specific image processing commands with it. To do this, right-click the folder concerned and click the **Properties** option. Click the **Customize** tab and open the **Use this folder type as a template** list.

▦ Click the **Pictures** or **Photo Album** option.

▦ Click the **OK** button.

B-Viewing a picture

▦ Click the **start** button then the **My Pictures** option.

If your images are stored in another folder, use the Windows Explorer to access that folder.

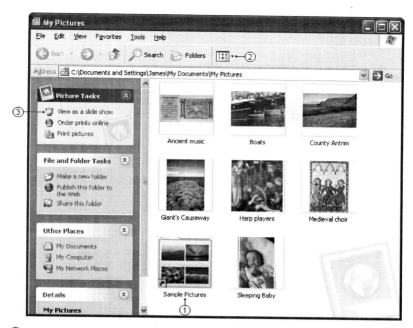

① If necessary, double-click the name of the folder (or sub-folder) that contains your pictures.

② Change the view by choosing one of the six view options.

③ Click to view the pictures in your folder as a slide show: click the **View as a slide show** link.

If you do not select anything or select just one picture, the slide show will display all the pictures in the folder, one after the other. If you select at least two pictures in the folder, the slide show will include only those pictures you have selected.

▓ Use the tools on the following bar to start or pause the slide show, to go to the previous or next picture, or to close the slide show view:

If this toolbar is not visible, move the mouse pointer to make the bar appear at the top right of the screen.

C-Printing a picture

▓ Open the **My Pictures** folder from the **start** menu and, if necessary, click the name of the folder that contains your pictures.

You do not need to open it or select anything.

▓ Click the **Print pictures** link in the **Picture Tasks** frame.

▓ In the **Photo Printing Wizard** window that opens, click the **Next** button.

MULTIMEDIA APPLICATIONS

Selected pictures have a tick next to them.

▓ To select or deselect a specific picture, click the check box in the top right-hand corner of the picture concerned.

▓ When you have selected the pictures, click the **Next** button.

▓ Open the **What printer do you want to use?** list and choose the printer you require.

▓ Click the **Printing Preferences** button to define settings such as the paper quality: these settings will vary according to the printer model you are using.

▓ Click the **Next** button.

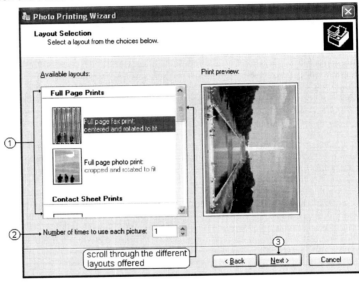

① Click the layout you require.

② Specify the number of copies of each picture you require.

③ Click this button.

▓ Click the **Finish** button.

D-Sending a photo by e-mail

▓ Open the **My Pictures** folder from the **start** menu then, if necessary, open the folder containing the picture you want to send by e-mail.

▓ Click the required photo to select it.

▓ Click the **E-mail this file** link.

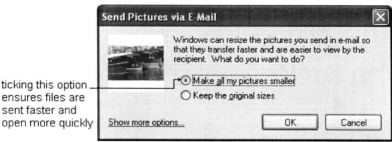

ticking this option
ensures files are
sent faster and
open more quickly

Windows can resize the pictures you send in e-mail so that they transfer faster and are easier to view by the recipient. What do you want to do?

- Make all my pictures smaller
- Keep the original sizes

Show more options...

OK   Cancel

▓ Click the **OK** button.

Your default e-mail application will open. Windows XP generates a (smaller) file and attaches it to a new mail message.

▓ Give the recipients, a message subject and write your text then send the message.

4.1 Toolbars

A-Managing the taskbar

▦ If you cannot move the taskbar, it is probably locked. To unlock it, right-click an empty space on it, and remove the tick from the **Lock the Taskbar** option.

▦ To move the taskbar, first check that it is not locked, then drag the taskbar to another side of the screen.

▦ To change the height (or width) of the taskbar, point to its top border (or to its right, left or bottom border according to its position) then drag.

▦ To manage the display of the taskbar, right-click an empty area of the taskbar then click the **Properties** option.

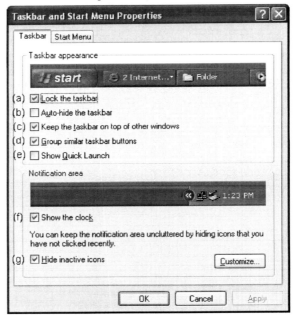

▦ Activate (or deactivate) the following options to suit your needs:

(a)   activate this option if you do not want to be able to move the taskbar.

(b)   activate this option to reduce the taskbar to a thin line at the bottom of the screen: it reappears when you point to this line.

(c)   activate this option if you want the taskbar to stay visible when an application runs in full-screen mode.

(d) activate this option to group files of the same application on one button. You can click this button to open its list and choose the file you want to view.

(e) activate this option to display the **Quick Launch** bar in the taskbar: you can show the desktop or start an application directly from this bar.

(f) activate this option to show the time in the **notification area** to the right of the taskbar: when you point to the time, the current date appears in a ScreenTip.

(g) activate this option to hide unused icons in the **notification area** to the right of the taskbar: the ◀ button displays these hidden icons.

B-Showing/hiding a toolbar

▓ Right-click an empty space on the taskbar.

▓ Activate the **Toolbars** option and activate one of the toolbars offered.

⇨ *By default, only the **Language** bar is shown. When only part of a toolbar is shown, access the hidden icons by clicking the* ≫ *button that appears on the right of the toolbar.*

C-Moving a toolbar/a tool on a bar

▓ If necessary, unlock the taskbar (cf. 4.1 - A - Managing the taskbar).

▓ Point to the vertical line at the beginning of the toolbar you wish to move.

The mouse pointer becomes a black two-headed arrow.

▓ On the taskbar, drag it to the required place.

If you move a toolbar onto the desktop, it appears in its own separate window.

▓ To move a tool button, point to the tool you wish to move and drag it left or right to the required position on the toolbar.

A thick black line indicates the tool's new position.

D-Creating/deleting a toolbar

You can create two types of toolbar: one showing the contents of a folder, the other showing the contents of a Web site (in this case you should increase the height of the taskbar).

▓ Right-click an empty space on the taskbar.

▓ Activate **Toolbars** then the **New Toolbar** option.

CONFIGURATION

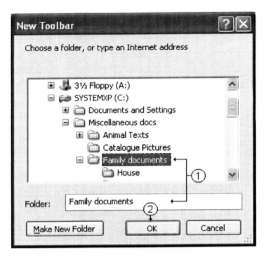

① Select a folder or enter an Internet address.

② Click to confirm the new bar.

⇨ *To hide (and at the same time delete) a created toolbar, right-click the taskbar, choose **Toolbars** and deactivate the option corresponding to its name in the shortcut menu.*

E-Creating a shortcut in a toolbar

A shortcut represents an object such as a folder, an application or a file. It can be inserted in a toolbar, so that you can access the file, folder or application quickly, directly from the toolbar.

▓ Go into the Explorer window and select the folder containing the file, program or folder concerned.

▓ Drag the icon of the folder, application or file directly onto the appropriate place on the desired toolbar (which must, of course, be visible).

shortcut to Paint⌐   ⌐shortcut to a folder

shortcut to a Word document

⇨ *To start the application symbolised by the shortcut or to open the represented folder or file, click the shortcut icon.*

4.2 Start menu

A- Customising the start menu

▓ Right-click the **start** button and choose the **Properties** option.

The Start Menu page from the Taskbar and Start Menu Properties dialog box appears on the screen.

▓ To give the **start** menu the same look as in previous versions of Windows (Windows 98, Windows 2000, etc), tick the **Classic Start menu** option.

If you choose this option, the procedure for customising the start menu will be quite different: this procedure in not covered in this book. This chapter deals only with the Windows XP style of start menu (Start menu option).

▓ Click the **Customize** button.

Start menu version:

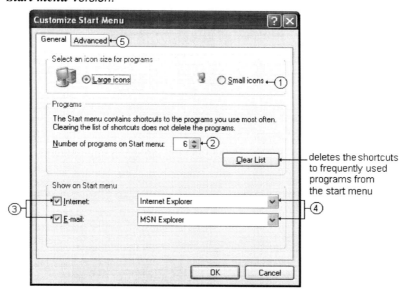

① To change the size of the icons associated with the names of frequently used programs, activate this option.

② To modify the number of frequently used programs that appear in the **start** menu, select or enter a new number.

③ To display the icons for your **Internet** browser and your **E-mail** application in the **start** menu, make sure the corresponding options are ticked.

④ To change the programs used as the **Internet** browser and for **E-mail**, open the drop-down list on the appropriate option and choose the name of the program that you want to use.

⑤ Click this tab.

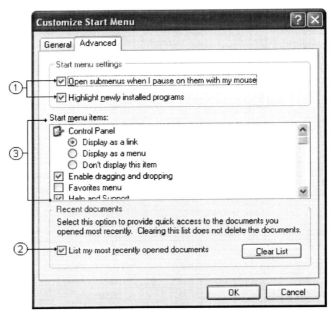

① If Windows must **Open submenus when I pause on them with my mouse**, and/or **Highlight newly installed programs** in the **All Programs** list in the **start** menu, tick the corresponding option.

② To add the **My Recent Documents** folder to the **start** menu, and have fast access to the last 15 documents opened, tick this option.

③ To choose the elements displayed in the **start** menu, tick the corresponding options; for some of these options, Windows gives you two choices:

Display as a link   the item will appear in the form of a link in the start menu.

Display as a menu   the item will appear as a menu within the **start** menu (a black arrow appears to the right of such items).

B-Clearing the list of My Recent Documents

*The **My Recent Documents** menu contains the names of the last fifteen files you have used.*

▓ Right-click the **start** button and take the **Properties** option.

▓ Click the **Customize** button then the **Advanced** tab.

▓ Click the **Clear List** button in the **Recent documents** frame, then click **OK** twice.

C-Inserting an option into a personal start menu

*You can add options to the **start** menu that will give you easier access to your favourite applications and to your personal folders and work files. These shortcuts will not appear in the **start** menus of other users on the computer.*

▓ **start - All Programs - Accessories - Windows Explorer**

▓ Select the file, the program file or the folder that you want to insert into the **start** menu then drag that item onto the **start** button on the taskbar.

▓ When the transparent image of the item appears on the **start** button, release the mouse button.

⇨ *There is another technique you can use to insert a program into the top of the **start** menu: right-click the application file or icon in the Windows Explorer, on the desktop or in the **All Programs** list in the **start** menu then choose the **Pin to Start menu** option.*

⇨ *If the item you want to put into the **start** menu has an icon on the Windows desktop, you can insert that item into the top of the **start** menu (which contains your permanent items) by dragging the icon from the desktop onto the **start** button.*

D-Inserting an option into the start menu's All Programs list

*You can add an option to your own **All Programs** list, but if you have a Computer administrator account, you can also add options to the **All Programs** list for one or all other users.*

▓ Right-click the **start** button.

▓ Click the **Explore All Users** option if you want to add the option to the **All Programs** menu for another or all the other users of the computer; click the **Explore** option if you want to add the option to your **All Programs** menu.

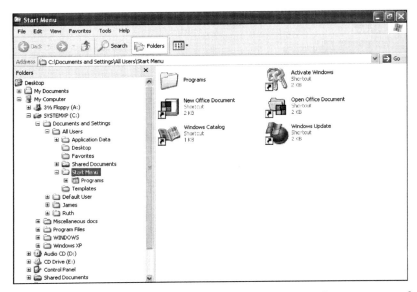

In the **Folders** bar, you can see the hierarchy of the **Documents and Settings** folder, in which you can find the folder for each user of the computer and the **All Users** folder, which is common to all the users. If you clicked the **Explore All Users** option, the **Start Menu** folder of the **All Users** folder will be selected. If you clicked the **Explore** option, the **Start Menu** folder of the active user will be selected.

- To insert an option into the top part of the **All Programs** menu, select the **Start Menu** folder for the user concerned within the **Documents and Settings** folder (for example, C:\Documents and Settings\James\Start Menu) or select the **Start Menu** folder in the **All Users** folder if you want to insert the option in the **All Programs** menu for all the computer's users.

- To insert an option in the lower part of the **All Programs** menu, select the **Programs** folder for the user concerned within the **Start Menu** folder. To insert an option in the **All Programs** menu for all the computer's users, select the **Programs** subfolder in the **Start Menu** folder that is in the **All Users** folder.

- To insert an option in one of the submenus of the **All Programs** menu, select the folder for the submenu corresponding to the user in question: this will be within that user's **Programs** folder. If you want to insert the option into a submenu of the **All Programs** menu for all the computer's users, go to the **All Users** folder and select the subfolder for the submenu concerned within the **Programs** folder.

- Click the **File** menu, point to the **New** option and take the **Shortcut** option.

- Give the location of the file, folder or program for which you are creating the shortcut by either entering the file path in the **Type the location of the item** box or by clicking the **Browse** button to select it in the hierarchy.
- Click the **Next** button then, if you wish, change the name of the shortcut.
- Click the **Finish** button.

  The shortcut can be seen in the right hand pane of the Explorer.

- Close the Windows Explorer window by clicking the ⊠ button.

⇨ *If you want Windows to open a file, folder or application automatically when you log on, you can do one of two things: you can create a shortcut to the file, folder or application in the **Startup** folder of the user concerned or, if you want to open the file/folder/application when any user logs on to the computer, you can create the shortcut in the **Startup** folder within the **All Users** folder.*

E-Removing options from the start menu

- Display the option you want to remove: click the **start** button, point to the **All Programs** menu then, if necessary, point to the submenu in which you inserted the option.
- Right-click the option you want to remove.
- Click the **Remove from This List** option (if the option is in a personal start menu) or the **Delete** option (if the option is in the **All Programs** menu or one of its submenus).

  When you remove an item from your personal start menu, no confirmation is required; the deletion is instantaneous.

  *When you remove an item from the **All Programs** menu or one of its submenus, you will see a message asking for confirmation.*

- Depending on the message, click the **Yes** button or the **Delete Shortcut** button.

CONFIGURATION

4.3 Interface

A-Creating a shortcut on the desktop

*A **shortcut** represents an object such as a drive, a folder, a file or an application. You can include a shortcut on your desktop to make the drive, folder, file or application readily available.*

▦ Open the Windows Explorer, but reduce the size of the window to show part of your desktop in the background.

▦ Drag the icon of the file, program or folder onto the desktop.

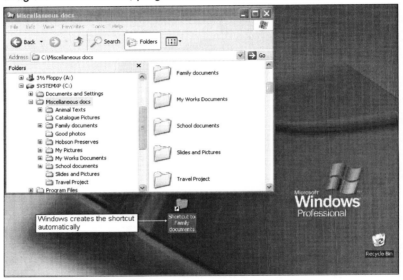

▦ To start the associated application or open the associated drive/folder/file, double-click the shortcut on the desktop.

▦ To rename your shortcut, right-click it, choose the **Rename** option and enter the new name for the shortcut.

⇨ *To delete a shortcut, right-click its icon and click the **Delete** option, or select it and press the ⌨Del key. Confirm your action.*

⇨ *To create a desktop shortcut to an option in a personal **start** menu (the top left part of the **start** menu), open the **start** menu and drag the item concerned onto the desktop.*

⇨ *To create a desktop shortcut to an item in the **All Programs** menu or one of its submenus, open the **start** menu, point to the **All Programs** menu (and one of its submenus if required) then right-click the item concerned. Click the **Create Shortcut** option and drag the shortcut that appears at the bottom of the list onto the desktop.*

B-Managing the display of icons on the desktop

▓ To move an icon, point to it and drag it to its new position.

▓ To sort the icons on your desktop, right-click an empty area of the desktop and point to the **Arrange Icons By** option. Click an option according to how you want to sort your icons (**Name**, **Size**, **Type** or date last **Modified**).

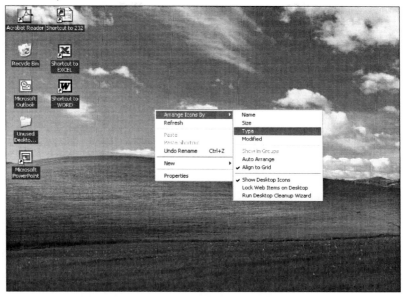

▓ To change the name of an icon, select it, click its name again then modify the text and confirm by pressing the [Enter] key.

▓ To change the appearance of certain icons, right-click an empty space on the desktop, and click the **Properties** option. Click the **Desktop** tab then click the **Customize Desktop** button. Select the item whose icon you want to change then click the **Change Icon** button. Select a new icon then click **OK** three times.

▓ To show the **My Documents**, **My Computer**, **My Network Places** or **Internet Explorer** icons on the desktop, right-click the desktop, choose **Properties - Desktop** tab, click the **Customize Desktop** button and tick the icon options.

⇨ *The **Restore Default** button in the **Desktop Items** dialog box can be used to retrieve the default icon used for the selected item.*

CONFIGURATION

C-Changing the desktop's background

▨ Right-click an empty space on the desktop and click the **Properties** option.

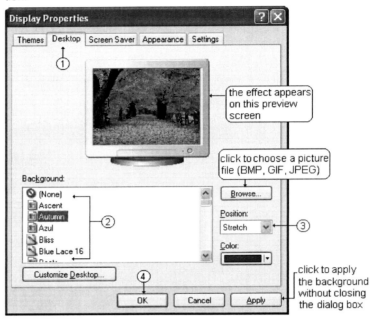

① Click this tab.

② Select the image you wish to display over the desktop.

③ Choose how to arrange the image on the background:

Center	The single image appears at the centre of the screen.
Tile	The image is duplicated until it fills the whole screen.
Stretch	The single image is stretched to fill the whole screen.

④ Click to confirm.

D-Choosing a screen saver

▨ Right-click an empty space on the desktop then click the **Properties** option.

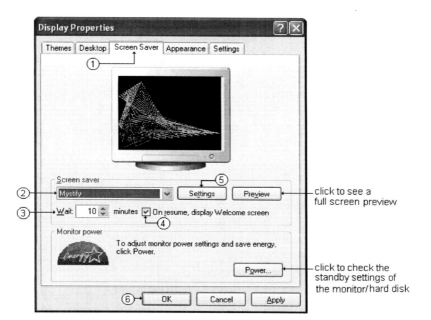

click to see a full screen preview

click to check the standby settings of the monitor/hard disk

① Click this tab.

② Select the screen saver from this list box.

③ Specify, in minutes, how long the screen should be inactive before the screen saver starts.

④ If you want Windows to return to its Welcome screen (where you log on) when you re-activate the computer, tick this option.

⑤ Click this button to set parameters for the chosen screen saver (if you have chosen **3D Text** for example, you can enter the text you want the screen saver to display) then click **OK**.

⑥ Click to confirm.

⇨ *Do not confuse the screen saver with the screen standby feature, whose main goal is to save energy.*

E-Defining the appearance of windows and dialog boxes

▨ Right-click an empty space on the desktop then click the **Properties** option.

▨ Click the **Appearance** tab.

▨ Select the style you want to use for **Windows and buttons** from the list of the same name.

▨ In the **Color scheme** box, select the scheme you want to use.

▨ Select the **Font size** you want to use in your windows.

▨ Click the **Effects** button to define visual effects for menus, icons and fonts then confirm these settings by clicking **OK**.

CONFIGURATION

- Click the **Advanced** button to customise the appearance of the windows, menus, fonts or icons.
- To change the colour of one of the desktop items, first select the item concerned from the **Item** list then select the colour(s) you want to apply using one of the **Color** lists.
- To change the size of one of the desktop items, first select the item concerned from the **Item** list then choose its new size in the **Size** list.
- If the item you choose has text, you can modify the text's **Font, Size, Color** and attributes: bold characters (B) and or italics (_I_).
- Click the **OK** button in the **Advanced Appearance** dialog box.
- Click **OK** again.

F- Setting screen display parameters

- Right-click an empty space on the desktop and click the **Properties** option.
- Click the **Settings** tab.
- Select the number of colours used on the screen from the **Color quality** list.

  The options in this list are directly linked to the characteristics of your graphics card.

- If required, you can change the screen resolution by dragging the **Screen resolution** slider.

  The screen resolution determines the number of pixels displayed over the width and height of the screen. A large number of pixels means that the elements on the screen are smaller so you can display more elements at any given time. The various resolutions available are again linked to your graphics card.

- Click **OK**.

⇨ _Some games or other applications work better with a different configuration than that offered by the **Display Properties** dialog box. It is possible to adjust the settings (cf. 1.1 - E - Starting an application)._

G- Associating sounds with events

- In the **start** menu, click **Control Panel** then the **Sounds, Speech and Audio Devices** link then click the **Change the sound scheme** link.

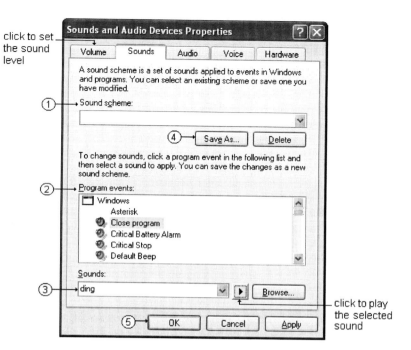

click to set the sound level

① If necessary, select a scheme from this list.

② Select the event to which you want to apply a sound.

③

⑤

click to play the selected sound

Events that already have a sound allocated are marked with a icon.

① If necessary, select a scheme from this list.

Windows comes with a sound scheme called **Windows Default**. This scheme contains a set of sounds assigned to different events. You can modify this sound scheme or create a new one.

② Select the event to which you want to apply a sound.

③ Choose the sound file that must run when your chosen event occurs, or choose the **None** option to apply no sound to this event.

④ If you have modified the sounds that are applied (or not applied) to the events but you want to keep the former sound scheme, click this button. Enter a name for the new scheme (this saves it under another name) and click **OK**.

⑤ Click to confirm.

⇨ *To delete a sound scheme, select it in the **Sound scheme** list and click the **Delete** button.*

⇨ *If you like, you can record your own sounds using the Windows **Sound Recorder** (start button - **All Programs - Accessories - Entertainment**).*

CONFIGURATION

H-Creating your own desktop theme

*The general look of your desktop (including its background, screen saver, windows, buttons, fonts and sounds) is called its theme. Windows XP provides a **Windows XP** and a **Windows Classic** theme. You can use these standard themes as a basis for creating new themes.*

▓ Right-click an empty space on the desktop then click the **Properties** option.

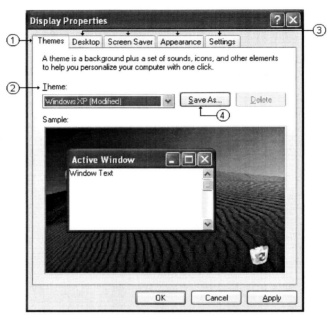

① Click this tab.

② Select the theme you want to use as a basis for a new theme.

③ Use the various options under these tabs to redefine the appearance of your desktop.

*If necessary, you can include a sound scheme in your new theme (cf. 4.3 - G - Associating sounds with events), while keeping the **Display Properties** dialog box open.*

*You can also include a different mouse pointer (using **start - Control Panel - Printers and Other Hardware - Mouse**) while the **Display Properties** dialog box is still open.*

*If any other dialog boxes you have opened to define your new theme are hiding the **Display Properties** dialog box, you can redisplay this dialog box by right-clicking an empty space on your desktop and clicking the **Properties** option.*

④ Click this button to confirm.

- If necessary, change the folder that must contain your new theme (by default, Windows stores your themes in your **My Documents** folder).
- To replace an existing theme, enter its exact name in the **File name** box. To create a new theme, enter a name that does not already exist.
- Click the **Save** button.

  If you chose to replace an existing theme, Windows tells you that it already exists and asks you to confirm your action.

- Click **Yes** to replace the existing theme.

⇨ *To delete a theme you have created, display the Display Properties dialog box (right-click an empty space on your desktop, then choose Properties option, Themes tab) select the theme you want to delete from the Theme list then click the Delete button. You cannot delete the standard Windows XP and Windows Classic themes.*

I- Changing the system date and time

Only users with Computer administrator accounts can change the system date and time.

- Click the **start** button, followed by **Control Panel**. Click the **Date, Time, Language, and Regional Options** link then click the **Date and Time** link.

  Alternatively, you can double-click the time displayed on the taskbar.

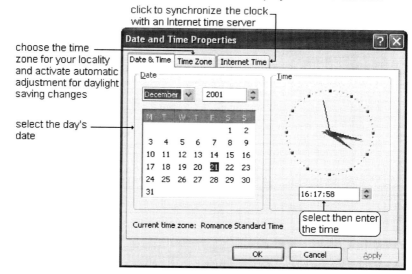

J- Defining regional options for dates and numbers

░ Click the **start** button and open the **Control Panel**. Click the **Date, Time, Language, and Regional Options** link then the **Change the format of numbers, dates, and times** link.

░ On the **Regional Options** page, select the country whose settings you want to use.

░ Click the **Customize** button.

░ Use the **Numbers** page to define the format of numerical values in Windows applications.

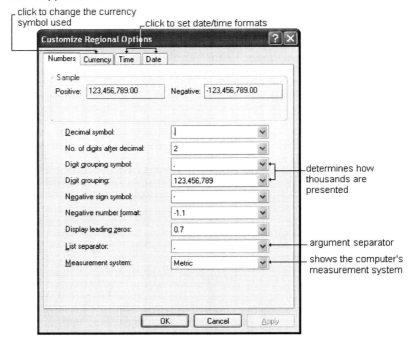

click to change the currency symbol used

click to set date/time formats

determines how thousands are presented

argument separator

shows the computer's measurement system

K-Defining how the mouse reacts

▓ Click the **start** button and open the **Control Panel**. Click the **Appearance and Themes** link then the **Mouse Pointers** link that is in the **See Also** frame at the left of the screen.

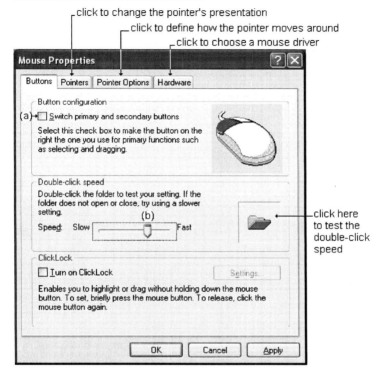

click to change the pointer's presentation
click to define how the pointer moves around
click to choose a mouse driver

click here
to test the
double-click
speed

By default, the left mouse button is the primary button and the right is the secondary button. The primary button is used to make selections and choose menu options. The right mouse button opens shortcut menus.

▓ If you are left-handed, you may want to tick (a) to switch over the primary and secondary buttons.

▓ Set the speed of the mouse double-click by dragging the slider (b) towards **Slow** or **Fast**. The closer it is to **Fast**, the shorter the time allowed between each click.

⇨ *If your mouse has a wheel, the options on the **Wheel** page can be used to define how far you can scroll when you move the mouse wheel.*

CONFIGURATION

L- Managing fonts

▓ Go into the **Control Panel**, click the **Appearance and Themes** link then the **Fonts** link in the **See Also** frame at the left of the screen.

▓ You can use the options in the **View** menu to define how the fonts are listed in the window. The **List Fonts By Similarity** option displays a degree of similarity in relation to a reference font that you can select.

▓ Double-click the icon or name of a font to open a window containing sample text using the font in different sizes (the **Print** button prints the contents of this window).

▓ To delete fonts, select the font(s) and press ⌨Del.

▓ To install new fonts, use the **File - Install New Font** command. Select a drive then the folder containing the font files. Select the fonts you wish to install using the ⌨Ctrl or ⌨⇧Shift keys if necessary then click **OK**.

M-Using the Desktop Cleanup Wizard

By default, Windows XP removes any icons from the desktop that have not been used for at least 60 days.

Deactivating/activating automatic desktop cleanup

▓ **start** button - **Control Panel** - **Appearance and Themes** - **Display**

▓ Click the **Desktop** tab then the **Customize Desktop** button.

▓ To turn off the Cleanup Wizard, deactivate the **Run Desktop Cleanup Wizard every 60 days** option. Tick to activate the Wizard if it has been deactivated.

Cleaning up the desktop manually

You can delete icons from the desktop yourself. When you do this, the removal is not permanent: Windows merely transfers the icons to the ***Unused Desktop Shortcuts*** *folder so they can be easily placed on the desktop again if need be.*

▓ **start** button - **Control Panel** - **Appearance and Themes** - **Display**

▓ Click the **Desktop** tab then the **Customize Desktop** button.

▓ Click the **Clean Desktop Now** button, then **Next**.

▓ Tick the **Shortcuts** you want to remove from the desktop.

▓ Click the **Next** button.

▓ To modify this list, click the **Back** button or to confirm the deletion, click the **Finish** button.

Reactivating deleted shortcuts

▨ Double-click the ▨ **Unused Desktop Shortcuts** icon on the desktop.

▨ Click the icon you wish to replace on the desktop then click **Move this file.**

▨ Click the **Desktop** as the file location and click **Move** to confirm.

⇨ *A **Shortcut** icon is managed as any other file, so you can also move it using the traditional dragging or "cut-and-paste" techniques (cf. 2.2 - F - Moving files or folders).*

5.1 System tools

A- Defragmenting a volume

To defragment a drive, you must be logged on as a Computer adminis-trator.

Defragmenting a disk groups together the data on contiguous tracks on the disk, so that data access is easier and faster.

▓ **start** - **All Programs** - **Accessories** - **System Tools** - **Disk Defragmen-ter** or, from the Windows Explorer, right-click the disk drive concerned, choose **Properties** and click the **Defragment Now** button on the **Tools** page.

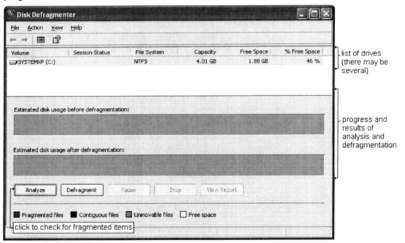

▓ Click the **Defragment** button.

Even if the disk has already been analysed, the Defragmenter runs an analysis.

Defragmenting a disk can take up to one hour, depending on the state of the disk.

While it is being defragmented, you can still use your computer to per-form other tasks, although it may be slower than usual. You can tempora-rily pause the defragmentation process by clicking the Pause button.

▓ When defragmentation is finished, click the **View Report** button or the **Close** button.

B-Restoring the system

Restoring the system means returning to a prior system configuration based on restore points: this allows you to cancel changes made to your computer without losing your work. To use these tools, you must be logged on as the Computer administrator.

Activating system restore

▓ **start** - **Control Panel** - **Performance and Maintenance** - **System**

▓ Click the **System Restore** tab then make sure the **Turn off System Restore on all drives** option is not active.

Creating a restore point

▓ **start** - **All Programs** - **Accessories** - **System Tools** - **System Restore**

You can also get to the System Restore window using start - Help and Support - Undo changes to your system with System Restore link.

▓ Activate the **Create a restore point** option and click the **Next** button.

▓ Enter a **Restore point description** in the appropriate text box and click **Create**.

▓ Click the **Close** button.

Restoring your system

▓ Close the open applications and log off all other users.

▓ **start** - **All Programs** - **Accessories** - **System Tools** - **System Restore**

▓ Activate the **Restore my computer to an earlier time** option then click the **Next** button.

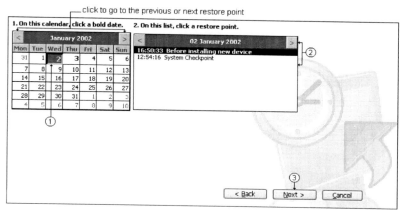

① On the calendar, click the date in bold that contains the restore point on which you wish to base your system restoration.

② Select an automatic or manual restore point from which the system will be restored.

③ Click this button.

▨ If necessary, save and close all your files then close any open application and click **Next**.

When the restore is finished, your system restarts automatically.

▨ If necessary, log on again from the Windows Welcome screen.

The System Restore tool displays a message to tell you your system has been successfully restored.

▨ Click **OK**.

Cancelling a system restoration

▨ **start - All Programs - Accessories - System Tools - System Restore**

▨ Activate the **Undo my last restoration** option and click the **Next** button.

▨ If necessary, save and close all your files and close any open applications.

▨ Click **Next**.

When the system restore cancellation is finished, your system restarts automatically.

▨ If necessary, log on again from the Windows Welcome screen.

*The System Restore tool displays an **Undo Complete** message to tell you that the last system restoration was successfully cancelled.*

▨ Click **OK**.

⇨ *Another way of cancelling a system restoration is to perform another restoration using a restore point occurring before the one you wish to cancel.*

C-Displaying the system information

The system information can supply the network administrator with useful information about the configuration of your computer.

▨ **start - All Programs - Accessories - System Tools - System Information**

The system information is organized in hierarchical form and is divided into different categories called nodes.

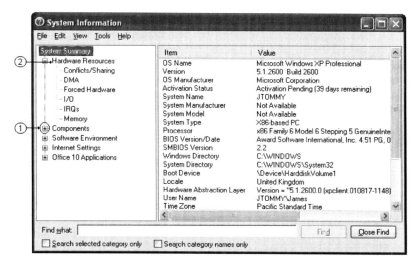

① Expand a branch if necessary by clicking the + sign in front of the node name

② Click the node's name to view its contents in the right hand pane of the window.

*The **System Summary** node displays information pertaining to the computer and the version of the Windows XP operating system. The **Hardware Resources** node shows settings specific to the hardware being used. The **Conflicts/Sharing** branch can tell you which devices share resources or are in conflict. The **Components** node contains information about your configuration of Windows and can also indicate the status of any device drivers, network or multimedia applications. The **Software Environment** node gives an overview of the software loaded in the computer. The **Internet Settings** node displays information concerning Internet Explorer 6. The **Office 10 Applications** node displays information specific to each Microsoft Office application installed on your computer.*

⇨ *You can print the system information contained in a particular category by selecting that category and using **File - Print**.*

Looking for system data

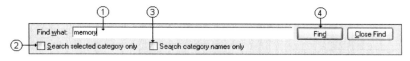

① Enter the keyword(s) corresponding to the system information you are looking for.

② If necessary, activate this option to search only the selected category and its subcategories.

③ If required, activate this option if you wish to search only the names of categories and subcategories in the hierarchy.

④ Click to start the search.

▓ Continue searching with the **Find** button or click **Close Find** to interrupt the search.

D-Cleaning up a disk

This tool detects and removes temporary files in order to free space on your hard disk (or on a floppy disk).

▓ **start - All Programs - Accessories - System Tools - Disk Cleanup**, or from the Windows Explorer, right-click the disk drive, choose **Properties** and the **General** tab and click **Disk Cleanup**.

▓ If you used the start menu and not the Windows Explorer, specify which drive you want to clean up: **A:** (floppy disk), **C:** (hard disk), etc.

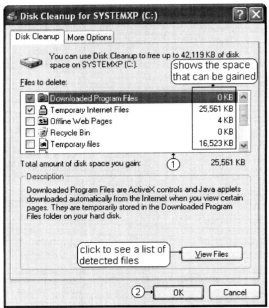

① Select the type of file you wish to erase by clicking the corresponding check box.

② Click to erase the selected files from the disk then confirm the file deletion.

E-Using the task scheduler

Scheduled tasks allow you to programme the automatic execution of certain applications. The Scheduled Tasks utility opens at the same time as Windows and works in the background.

▓ **start - All Programs - Accessories - System Tools - Scheduled Tasks**

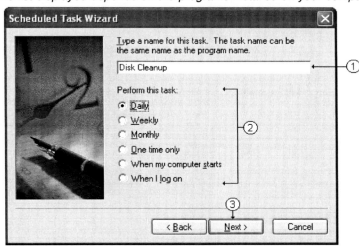

You can also use start - Control Panel - Performance and Mainte-nance - Scheduled Tasks.

Creating a scheduled task

▓ From the **Scheduled Tasks** window, double-click the **Add Scheduled Task** icon.

The Scheduled Task Wizard opens and offers to help you.

▓ Click the **Next** button.

▓ Select the program you want Windows to run automatically then click **Next**.

The list displayed depends on the programs installed on your computer.

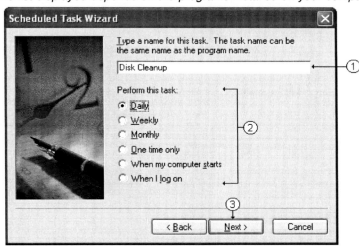

③ If required, specify a name for this new task.

② Choose how often you want this task to run.

③ Click to go to the next stop.

▓ Depending on the option chosen in the previous step, give the day, time or frequency of execution if necessary then click **Next**.

▓ If required, enter your user name and password then click **Next**.

▓ Click the **Finish** button.

The created task appears in the Scheduled Tasks window: the selected application will run automatically according to the settings you defined.

Modifying a scheduled task

▓ In the **Scheduled Tasks** window, click the task that you wish to modify.

▓ **File - Properties**

▓ Click one of the tabs:

Task to change the application that will run automatically.

Schedule to change the task's running frequency.

Settings to set customised options for the task.

Deleting a scheduled task

▓ Open the **Scheduled Tasks** window and select the task you wish to delete.

▓ Use **File - Delete** or click **Delete this item** in the **Folder Tasks** list on the left of the window.

You can also right-click the task you wish to remove and choose the **Delete** *option.*

▓ Confirm deleting the task.

Deactivating the task scheduler

To deactivate the task scheduler, you must be logged on as the Computer administrator.

▓ Go into the **Scheduled Tasks** window.

▓ **Advanced - Stop Using Task Scheduler**

The defined tasks will no longer run and the Scheduled Tasks utility will not start at the same time as Windows.

⇨ *To pause the scheduled tasks temporarily, open the* **Advanced** *menu and take the* **Pause Task Scheduler** *option; to resume using the scheduler, activate the* **Continue Task Scheduler** *in the* **Advanced** *menu.*

▓ 5.2 Installing

A-Installing a device

Overview

The procedures used for installing devices can vary; everything depends on the type and brand of the hardware you are installing and the type of connection.

You should follow the manufacturer's installation instructions to ensure that your device works properly.

Sometimes, Windows can detect and install a new device automatically when you connect it. Sometimes, Windows will not be able to recognise a new device, in which case you will need to install the device with the Add Hardware Wizard.

You may need to deactivate your antivirus software before installing the driver of the new device.

To install certain types of device, you need to be logged on as the Computer administrator (if the device driver is not installed on your computer, if your computer is connected to a network, and so on).

As this book cannot cover every conceivable situation, only the most likely installation procedures are described. Before installing, read on for an explanation of how digital signatures work.

Microsoft Windows XP and digitally signed drivers

To protect your system's integrity, Microsoft Windows XP checks that your hardware is compatible with your system. When you buy a device, you should make sure it is Designed for Microsoft Windows XP. This type of product has a digital signature, guaranteeing the compatibility of the product and your system.

During the installation procedure, Windows XP checks for the required digital signature.

If Windows XP recognises the connected device

Connect the new device to your computer (using a parallel, USB or serial port) and make sure it is correctly plugged in and switched on.

If Windows XP detects the connected device automatically, it will sometimes be able to work directly with the device without any further intervention on your part. If not, it offers a wizard to help you install it:

In this example, Windows XP has detected a newly-connected webcam but it needs extra information to be able to use the device. Because of this, it opens a wizard to help you complete the installation.

If you have an installation CD (or floppy disk) for the piece of hardware, insert it in the correct drive. Inserting a CD-ROM may open a new window: close this window to return to the **Found New Hardware Wizard** *window.*

- Ideally, you should use the **Install the software automatically** option, but if you want to choose which driver to use from a list or from a network location, you can use the **Install from a list or specific location** option.
- Click **Next**.

If Windows does not find the driver on your disk drives and if your computer is connected to the Internet, Windows will look for a driver on the Microsoft Web site. If it finds it, it copies the driver and installs it on your PC.

If you choose to select the driver from a list, or if there are several drivers available in the chosen location, Windows displays the various drivers and checks their digital signatures:

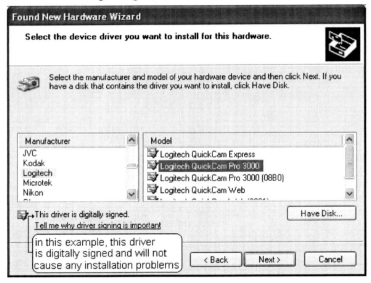

If the driver has not been designed for Windows XP (and so does not have a digital signature), the dialog box will tell you that the driver is not digitally signed. You can persist in trying to install the driver, but Windows XP will display a warning, as installing an unsigned driver may destabilise your system or prevent it from functioning properly. If you wish to continue the installation, despite the warnings given, Windows will take the precaution of memorising the configuration of your computer so it can restore it should any problems occur (cf. 5.1 - B - Restoring the system).

- In the list offered, pick the driver that corresponds to the hardware you are installing.
- Click the **Next** button.

▓ When the process is finished, click the **Finish** button.

Starting the Add Hardware Wizard

▓ Connect the new device to your computer, making sure it is correctly plugged in and switched on.

▓ **start** - **Control Panel** - **Printers and Other Hardware** - **Add Hardware**

▓ Click the **Next** button.

Windows searches for any new hardware you have connected.

▓ Continue with the installation, going through the steps described under the previous heading.

⇨ *If you want to install a printer by using a wizard, you can also use the **Add a printer** link (**Control Panel - Printers and Other Hardware**): follow the instructions provided.*

⇨ *To install a digital image device (scanner, digital camera or video camera) by using a wizard, you can also use the **Add an imaging device** link (**Control Panel - Printers and Other Hardware - Scanners and Cameras**): follow the instructions provided.*

⇨ *This Web site offers a large number of downloadable drivers: www.microsoft.com/downloads/search.asp.*

B-Installing/uninstalling an application

If you want to install, remove or modify certain applications, you must be logged on as a Computer administrator.

If the installation CD does not start automatically or if the application is on floppy disks, you will have to use the Windows installation features.

Installing an application

▓ **start** - **Control Panel** - **Add or Remove Programs**

▓ If necessary, click the **Add New Programs** button.

▓ Click the **CD or Floppy** button.

▓ As Windows prompts you to do, insert the first installation floppy disk or CD-ROM into the appropriate drive and click **Next**.

*Windows looks on the CD-ROM or floppy disk drive for the installation program then displays its name in the **Open** box. You can use the **Browse** button to search for the installation program manually.*

▓ Click the **Finish** button to start the installation process and follow the various steps right to the end.

⇨ *Once a program is installed, its name appears in the **start - All Programs** menu common to all users.*

⇨ *You can also use the **Run** command in the **start** menu to install a program from the CD-ROM or floppy disk drive.*

Modifying/removing an application

Before you modify or remove a program, make sure you are the only user currently logged on to the computer.

▓ **start - Control Panel - Add or Remove Programs**

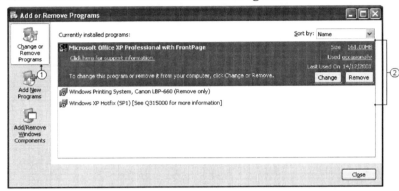

① Click this button.

② Click the row for the program you wish to change or remove.

*Depending on the application concerned, Windows offers either a single **Change/Remove** button, or two separate **Change** and **Remove** buttons. Be careful, as sometimes the **Change/Remove** button can simply remove the application, without offering you the option to change the application!*

▓ To modify a program, click the **Change/Remove** or **Change** button.

▓ To delete a program, click the **Change/Remove** or **Remove** button.

▓ Follow the instructions given to change or remove the application concerned.

C-Installing/uninstalling Windows components

You can remove some of the features added by default with Windows XP or add new ones.

▓ **start - Control Panel - Add or Remove Programs**

▓ Click the **Add/Remove Windows Components** button.

The list of components varies, depending on whether you are using Windows XP Professional or Home Edition. Components whose check boxes are ticked are installed and activated on your computer.

Windows Components Wizard

Windows Components
You can add or remove components of Windows XP.

To add or remove a component, click the checkbox. A shaded box means that only part of the component will be installed. To see what's included in a component, click Details.

Components:

☑ 📠 Accessories and Utilities	17.4 MB
☐ 📠 Fax Services	3.6 MB
☑ 📠 Indexing Service	0.0 MB
☑ 📠 Internet Explorer	0.0 MB
☐ 📠 Internet Information Services (IIS)	15.6 MB

Description: Includes Windows Accessories and Utilities for your computer.

Total disk space required: 0.0 MB
Space available on disk: 982.2 MB

[Details...]

[< Back] [Next >] [Cancel]

when you choose new additions Windows calculates the required space to install them

click to see what is included within a selected component

▦ To install an entire component (including all its parts), click to activate its check box. To uninstall a component, deactivate its check box.

▦ To select specific parts of the component you want to install or uninstall, click the component's name then click the **Details** button.

If the Details button does not appear, this means that the component has only one part.

▦ Tick or deactivate the check boxes of the component parts you wish to install or uninstall and click **OK**.

A light grey check box ☑ *indicates that not all the component's features have been selected.*

▦ Click the **Next** button.

Windows proceeds to install the components and displays the results of the operation.

▦ Click the **Finish** button.

D-Updating your computer with Windows Update

You may need to be logged on as a Computer administrator to carry out some of these tasks.

▦ Make sure your Internet connection is online.

▦ **start** - **Help and Support** - **Keep your computer up-to-date with Windows Update**

*After a few seconds, the Security **Warning** window appears and offers to install the Windows Update Control V4 application.*

▓ Click the **Yes** button to install the application that will analyse and memorise your computer's configuration.

Windows carries out its search: the time it takes depends on the speed of your Internet connection. If necessary, click Yes again on any security windows that appear.

▓ Click the **Scan for updates** link.

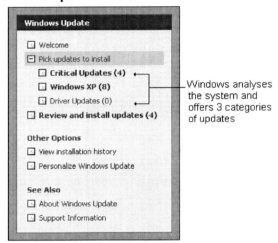

Windows analyses the system and offers 3 categories of updates

▓ Click the required update in the left pane to see details of its contents.

▓ To accept the update in question, click the **Add** button to put aside the update into a holding file. Repeat the operation for each update file that you wish to download.

Critical updates are retained automatically.

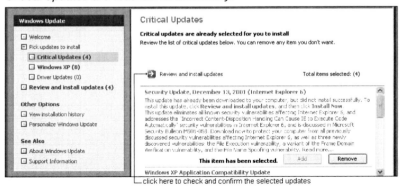

click here to check and confirm the selected updates

▓ Click the **Install Now** button to start the installation.

▓ Click the **I accept** button after you have read the licence agreement.

5.3 Windows Messenger 4.0

A-Looking at Windows Messenger 4.0

You can use the Windows Messenger application to exchange messages in real-time with other users on your intranet or on the Internet.

To use this system, you first have to identify yourself via your Microsoft .NET Passport. You can then log on to Windows Messenger and have live conversations with other users who are also identified and logged on.

To use Windows Messenger, you and your correspondents must have:

- *an Internet connection,*
- *a Microsoft Passport (cf. 1.3 - H - Creating a Microsoft .NET Passport),*
- *the Windows Messenger application installed on all computers (Windows XP installs this application automatically).*

B-Signing in to Messenger

▓ **start - All Programs - Windows Messenger**

▓ If you have only one Microsoft .NET Passport, or you want to activate the last one used, just wait and Windows will sign you in automatically.

▓ Otherwise, if you have several Passports and you want to use a different one from your last session, use **File - Sign out** then click **Or, click here to sign in as someone else**.

▓ If prompted to, identify yourself using the **E-mail address** and the **Password** of the passport you want to use (cf. 1.3 - H - Creating a Microsoft .NET Passport) then click **OK**.

▓ The **Windows Messenger** session opens automatically using data from the user passport.

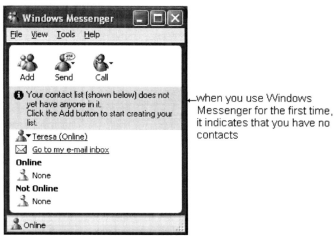

when you use Windows Messenger for the first time, it indicates that you have no contacts

▓ To hide this window, click the ✖ button or select **File - Close**.

Windows Messenger informs you that it will continue to run even though you have closed its window, so it is able to notify you as soon as you receive a message, (providing your Internet connection is active).

▓ Click the **OK** button.

The 🖼 *icon on the right of the taskbar symbolises the active Windows Messenger application.*

▓ To sign out of Windows Messenger, right-click the 🖼 taskbar icon then click the **Sign out** option.

If the Windows Messenger window is open you can also sign out using File - Sign out.

⇨ *To reactivate the Windows Messenger window while you are still signed in, double-click the* 🖼 *icon on the right of the taskbar (or click this icon to open its shortcut menu then click the* **Open** *option).*

C-Adding a contact to your list

▓ Sign in to Windows Messenger or open the Windows Messenger window.

▓ Click the ⟨Add⟩ button in the **Windows Messenger** window.

If you know your contact's e-mail address:

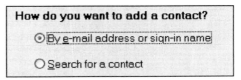

▓ Activate the **By e-mail address or sign-in name** option then click the **Next** button.

▓ In the text box provided, enter the full e-mail address of the person you want to add as a contact, then click **Next**.

Windows Messenger checks whether or not the contact you want to add has a Microsoft .NET Passport.

If the contact has a Microsoft .NET Passport, it adds him/her to your list:

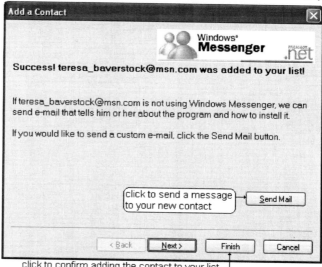

If your new contact does not have a Microsoft .NET Passport, Windows Messenger informs you that it cannot add your new contact to your list:

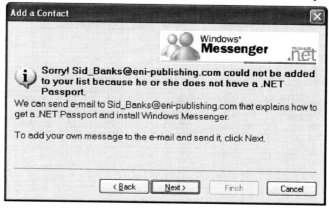

▓ To close this dialog box, without sending a message to this person, click the **Cancel** button. To send a message to suggest that he/she might like to create a Microsoft .NET Passport and use Windows Messenger, click the **Next** button.

■ If you click **Next**, the following dialog box appears:

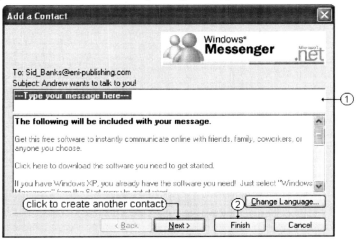

① Enter your message here.

② Click this button.

If you do not know your new contact's e-mail address

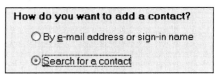

■ Activate the **Search for a contact** option then click the **Next** button.

■ Enter the **First Name**, the **Last Name** and possibly the **Country/Region** of the contact you want to add.

■ If necessary, open the **Search for this person at** list and choose to look for the person in the **Hotmail Member Directory** or in the **Address Book on this computer** then click the **Next** button.

The Address Book used for the search can be accessed using start - All Programs - Accessories - Address Book.

Windows Messenger shows its search results in a dialog box.

■ Select the name of the person concerned then click the **Next** button to check whether or not the person has a Microsoft .NET Passport.

■ If the person has a Microsoft .NET Passport, Windows Messenger offers to send him/her a message to explain how to install Windows Messenger and contact you. In this case, click the **Next** button to send the person a message or click the **Cancel** button if you decide you do not want to add this contact to your list.

■ If the person concerned does not have a Microsoft .NET Passport, you can send him/her a message to explain how to start exchanging messages via Windows Messenger.

⇨ *You can add up to 150 contacts to your list.*

⇨ *To delete a contact, right-click the name of the contact you want to re-move from your list then click the **Delete Contact** option (or press the* Del *key).*

⇨ *Windows Messenger users who are not on your contacts list can still con-tact you, unless you block them to prevent them from doing so.*

D-Blocking a contact

When you block a contact, you prevent him/her from contacting you di-rectly.

▧ Sign on or open the Windows Messenger window.

▧ To block or unblock a contact, right-click his/her name in the list and choose **Block** or **Unblock** accordingly.

⇨ *A blocked contact appears as follows:* ⊗ l.rice@eni.com (Blocked)

E-Communicating with Windows Messenger 4.0

▧ Sign on to Windows Messenger or open the Windows Messenger win-dow.

Sending an instant message to a contact

▧ Right-click the name of the person you want to contact, who can be either **Online** or **Not Online**.

▧ If the person is **Not Online**, Windows Messenger asks you to confirm that you want to send him/her mail by clicking the **Yes** button. In this case you can carry on creating your message. This procedure will vary according to your mailbox (msn.com, yahoo.com or excite.com, for example).

▧ If the person is **Online**, the **Conversation** window appears:

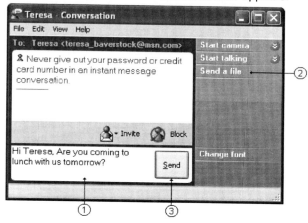

① Enter your message (of up to 400 characters) in the lower pane of the dialog box. You can include emoticons (little icons that express fee-lings, such as smiles, frowns, etc.) into your message. Look in the annexe at the end of this book to see a list of popular emoticons.

② To send a file with your message, click this link, select the file you want to send then click the **Open** button.

③ When your message is ready, click here.

The message you entered moves to the upper pane of the dialog box.

During your conversation, the status bar at the bottom of your dialog box tells you when your contact is typing a message:

Teresa is typing a message.

or the date and time of the last message you received:

Last message received on 30/05/2002 at 09:40.

⇨ *If you do not want to use emoticons, use **Tools - Options - Personal** tab and deactivate the **Show graphics (emoticons) in instant messages** op-tion, or from the **Conversation** window, using **Edit - Show Emoticons** (deactivate this option).*

Sending a message to a person who is not in your contacts list

▒ Click the button then choose the **Other** option.

Send an Instant Message

Enter the e-mail address of the person you want to send a message to.
Be sure to include the "@" portion of the name.

Sandra_Driscoll@eni-publishing.com

Example: someone@microsoft.com

Service: .NET Messenger Service

[OK]   [Cancel]

enter the e-mail address of your correspondent
(who must have a .NET Passport and Windows Messenger)

▒ Click **OK** to confirm.

The Conversation window opens.

▒ Enter your message then click the **Send** button.

Windows Messenger informs you if it is unable to contact your correspondent:

> ♣ The following message could not be
> delivered to all recipients:
>   Can we fix a time to discuss our new
>   project?

Calling another computer for an audio and/or video conversation

▨ Click the button.

▨ Point to the name of the person you wish to call (who must be online) and click the **Computer** option.

▨ In the **Conversation** window, click the **Start talking** button on the **Sidebar**.

If the sidebar does not appear, open it by clicking the Sidebar option in the View menu.

⇨ *If your computer is on a network using a firewall (a company intranet for example), you can talk to someone who is within the same firewall as you, but you will not be able to make a computer-to-computer call to someone outside that firewall.*

Inviting a friend

You can invite someone to play an online game or to use the Remote Assistance service.

▨ In the main window, right-click the contact you want to invite, point to the **Invite** option and choose the option that you wish to use.

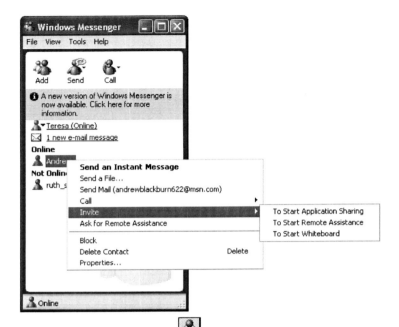

You can also click the **Invite** ( ) button on the **Conversation** window and point to the program you want to use.

Next, click the contact you want to invite.

*The **Conversation** window is active and you must wait for an answer from the contact you called.*

To cancel your call, press ⟨Alt⟩ **Q**.

⇨ *The programs you can use with invited contacts are displayed in the **In-vite** menu. Any game installed on your computer that uses the DirectPlayLobby interface will also appear in the **Invite** menu.*

Replying to an invitation

Depending on the type of invitation received, the message may differ but the reply principle remains the same.

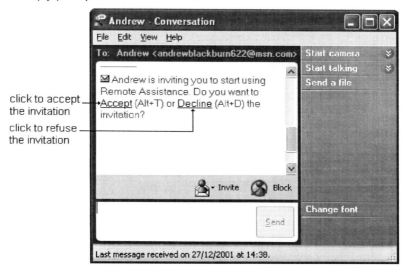

If you accept an invitation to play online, the game concerned starts automatically on your computer.

If you accept an invitation to use Remote Assistance, your computer will be connected to the other (remote) computer automatically (cf. 5.5 - Remote Assistance).

5.4 Networks and communication

A-Sharing a file/folder with other users

- start - **My Documents**
- If necessary, open the folder containing the item you wish to share.
- Click the file/folder to be shared then click the **Move this file** or **Move this folder** link.

└click to create a new folder or sub-folder

① Click **Shared Documents** if the item being shared is not a picture or a piece of music. If it is, click the **Shared Pictures** or **Shared Music** folder.

② Click this button.

B-Using My Network Places

My Network Places are shortcuts to computers, printers, Web servers and other types of shared network resources.

Creating a new network place

▓ **start - My Computer**

▓ Click **My Network Places** in the **Other Places** frame in the left pane of the window.

▓ Click the **Add a network place** link then click **Next**.

▓ Click **Choose another network location** then **Next**.

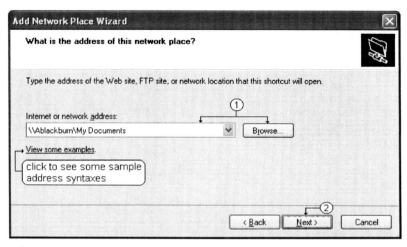

① Enter or browse for the address for which you want to create a shortcut.

② Click to go to the next step.

▓ If necessary, enter a more explicit name for the network place in the **Type a name for this network place** box.

▓ Click **Next** then **Finish**.

▓ To activate a network place, double-click it in the list of places (**start** - **My Network Places** or **My Computer** - **My Network Places**).

⇨ *To create a new network place towards a Web server, the server must be able to support My Network Places. My Network Places requires a Web Extender Client protocol and FrontPage extensions or a WebDAV protocol and Internet Information Services (IIS). Check with your Internet service provider or your network administrator that you have read and write per-missions for the Web server in question.*

⇨ *Once you have activated a network place, the* **My Network Places** *option appears in the* **start** *menu.*

⇨ *Once you access a shared network resource (such as a shared folder or a printer) using the* **Run** *command from the* **start** *menu, a corresponding shortcut is created automatically in* **My Network Places**.

C-Finding a computer on a network

▓ **start** - **Search** - **Computers or people** - **A computer on the network**

▓ In the **Computer name** box, give the name of the computer you want to find then click **Search**.

D-Activating/ deactivating an Internet firewall

A firewall is a security system that protects your computer by restricting the information that your computer or local network can communicate to the Internet and vice versa. Windows XP has an Internet firewall called ICF (Internet Connection Firewall).

To carry out these actions, you must be logged on as a Computer administrator.

▨ **start - Control Panel - Network and Internet Connections - Network Connections**

▨ Click the dial-up, local area or Internet connection concerned by the firewall then click the **Change settings of this connection** option.

▨ Click the **Advanced** tab.

tick this option to activate the firewall

▨ Click **OK** to confirm.

5.5 Remote Assistance

A-Overview

When connected via Remote Assistance to a friend's computer, you can see what is currently on his/her screen and you can discuss online what appears there. If the friend permits it, you can even control the remote computer with your own mouse and keyboard (and work on your own computer simultaneously).

To be able to use this feature, both users must have:

- Windows XP,

- an open Internet connection,

- Windows Messenger or a MAPI-compatible e-mail account (such as Outlook or Outlook Express),

- If you work on a local or business network (intranet), check with your network administrator that the firewall(s) in place will allow you to use remote assistance.

To ask for Remote Assistance, the user in difficulty has to "call" his/her friend via the Internet, using either the friend's e-mail address or his/her own Windows Messenger Passport.

B-Configuring your workstation

Before you invite a friend to connect to your computer with Remote Assistance and take control of it to solve a problem you are having, you should check some of your system settings to make sure Remote Assistance will work correctly.

▦ **start - Control Panel** - **Performance and Maintenance - System**

▦ Click the **Remote** tab.

▦ Make sure the **Allow Remote Assistance invitations to be sent from this computer** option is ticked.

▦ To authorise an outside correspondent to take control of your computer when the connection has been established, click the **Advanced** button and make sure the **Allow this computer to be controlled remotely** option is active.

▦ You can also, if necessary, **Set the maximum amount of time invitations can remain open**, using the associated drop-down lists.

▦ Click **OK** to confirm.

C-Establishing a connection with Windows Messenger

▦ Make sure your Internet connection is open.

▦ **start - Help and Support - Invite a friend to connect to your computer with Remote Assistance**

▦ Click the **Invite someone to help you** option.

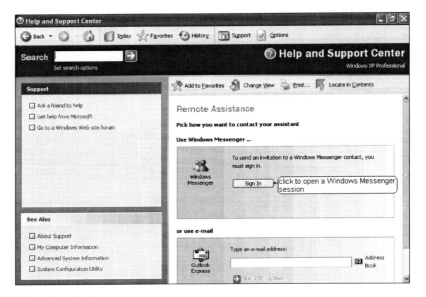

Asking for help

To use Windows Messenger, both the user in difficulty and their "Good Samaritan" friend must have a Windows Messenger Passport (cf. 1.3 - H - Creating a Microsoft .NET Passport).

▨ If you are not signed into Windows Messenger, click the **Sign In** button then enter the **E-mail address** and **Password** for your passport in the **.NET Messenger Service** dialog box then click **OK**.

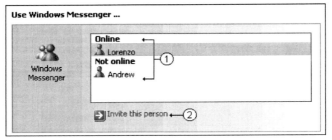

① Click the name of the person whom you wish to ask for help.

② Click to send the invitation.

▨ If the contact concerned is currently signed in to Windows Messenger the invitation is sent immediately. You should wait for your contact's reply.

▨ If the contact concerned is not signed in to Windows Messenger Windows XP will offer to send him/her an invitation by e-mail; in this case, click **OK**.

Enter your text inviting the friend to help you in the **Message** box and click **Continue**.

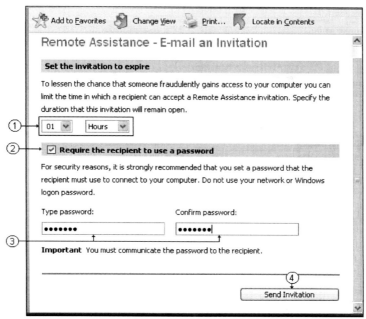

① If you wish, you can change the length of time during which this invitation is valid (the second list can be used to change the time unit).

② For tight security, you should tick this option.

③ Enter a password then confirm it. Your contact will have to enter this password to access your computer.

④ Click to send the invitation.

The message is sent using your default e-mail software (for example, Outlook). If you are using Outlook 2002 or Outlook Express 6, a window will tell you that a program is trying to access your e-mail address; click Yes or Send as necessary to continue sending the message.

The Remote Assistance feature tells you that the invitation has been sent. You now have to wait for your friend to reply.

Replying to an invitation

- If you are signed in to Windows Messenger, you receive this message:

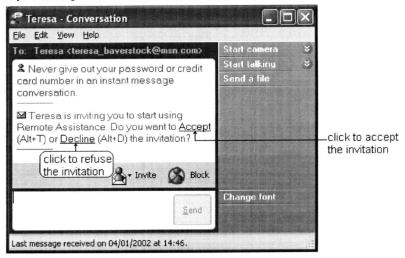

click to accept the invitation

- If you are not signed in to Windows Messenger, the invitation comes in the form of an attached file in an e-mail.
- In this case, open the invitation message, then double-click the name of the attachment (this may look like this: rcBuddy.MsRcIncident (1k)).
- Click the **Open** button on the **File Download** dialog box.
- If the invitation requires a password, this dialog box will appear:

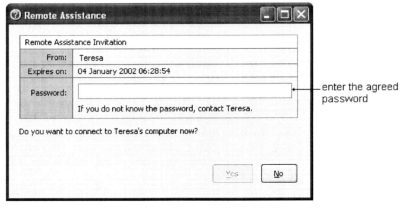

enter the agreed password

Windows XP connects to the computer that is having problems.

*For the connection to occur, the computer that was waiting for a reply has to authorise the other user to see its screen and converse with it; to do this, you should click **Yes** on this message:*

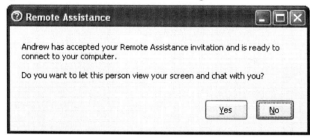

▨ Once the connection is established, the **Remote Assistance** window opens so you can see your friend's screen:

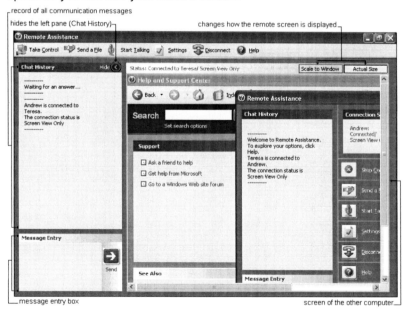

▨ For now you can only see your friend's screen and exchange messages and/or files with your friend. You cannot yet work directly on his/her computer.

The computer that asked for remote assistance will display this window:

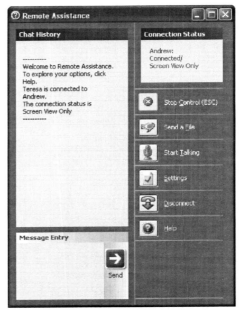

D-Establishing a connection via an e-mail address

▓ **start - Help and Support - Invite a friend to connect to your computer with Remote Assistance - Invite someone to help you**

Asking for help

▓ Make sure your Internet connection is open.

① Enter the e-mail address (a) of the person you want to ask for help, or choose it from an address book (b).

② Click here.

▓ Enter your text inviting the friend to help you in the **Message** box and click **Continue**.

- If you like, you can change the connection time allowed for this remote assistance invitation. By clicking the 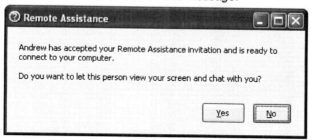 arrows you can specify the authorised number of **Minutes, Hours** and **Days.**

- It is recommended that you tick the **Require the recipient to use a password** option then enter the password in the **Type password** and **Confirm password** boxes. Your contact will also have to enter this password to access your computer.

- Click the **Send Invitation** button.

The message is sent using your default e-mail software (for example, Outlook). If you are using Outlook 2002 or Outlook Express 6, a window will tell you that a program is trying to access your e-mail addresses; click **Yes** *or* **Send** *as necessary to continue sending the message.*

The Remote Assistance feature tells you that the invitation has been sent. You now have to wait for your friend to reply.

Replying to an invitation

- If it is closed, open your e-mail application then open the invitation message. Next, double-click the name of the attached file (this may look like this: rcBuddy.MsRcIncident (1k)) then open it.

- Enter the password agreed on by you and the friend you are inviting then click **Yes.**

Windows XP connects to the computer that is having problems.

For the connection to occur, the computer that was waiting for a reply has to authorise the other user to see its screen and converse with it; to do this, the user should click **Yes** *on this message:*

*Once the connection is established, the **Remote Assistance** window opens so you can see your friend's screen.*

- For now you can only <u>see</u> your friend's screen and exchange messages and/or files with your friend.

E-Managing sent invitations

▨ **start** - **Help and Support** - **Invite a friend to connect to your computer with Remote Assistance**

▨ Click the **View invitation status** link.

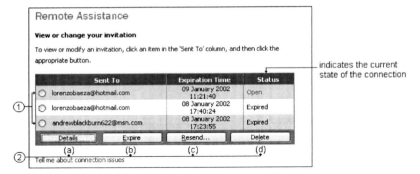

indicates the current state of the connection

① To intervene on an invitation, activate the corresponding option.

② Click this button:

(a) to show the personal details of the invited person, the invitation date, any message included with the invitation and whether or not password protection was added.

(b) to state that the time allocated to that invitation has expired.

(c) to send the invitation again with the same data (message, recipient etc).

(d) to delete the invitation from the list.

F-Helping a friend with Remote Assistance

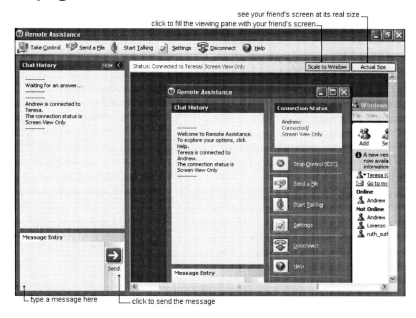

see your friend's screen at its real size

click to fill the viewing pane with your friend's screen

type a message here   click to send the message

Sending a file

▦ Click the [Send a File] button on the helper's computer.

▦ Enter the complete name (including its location) in the appropriate text box or click the **Browse** button to look for the file in your computer's hierarchy, or on your network.

▦ Click the **Send File** button.

The addressee receives notification that a file has been sent:

The addressee can click Save As to save the new file at the location he/she chooses in the Save As window.

A new window opens, offering to open the new, saved file immediately. If you want to do this, click Yes. If you want to open it at a later time, click No.

A message is returned to the sender to tell him/her that the addressee has accepted the file (whether it was opened or not).

As long as the addressee has not saved the file, the sender can stop the transfer by clicking the **Cancel** *button.*

Taking and releasing control of a remote computer

This feature allows the person you have asked for help to work directly on your computer. The helper uses his/her own keyboard and mouse to intervene on the files and system of the remote computer. While your computer is being controlled remotely, you can still work on it.

This feature works only if you authorise the third party to take control of your computer (cf. 5.5 - B).

▨ Set up a remote assistance connection.

▨ In the helper's **Remote Assistance** window, click the 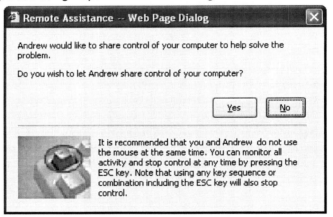 button.

The person being helped receives a message on his/her screen:

To allow the helper to take control of the computer, the user being helped should click the **Yes** *button.*

▨ Once the other user accepts the takeover, the helper is informed:

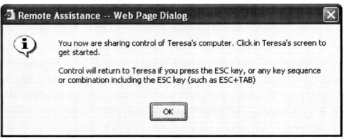

▨ Click **OK**.

The connection status changes slightly: Status: Connected to Teresa/ In Control .

- The helper now works on the remote computer as if it were his/her own computer.

- <u>On the computer receiving help</u>: to stop remote control of your computer, press Esc on the keyboard or click the **Stop Control (ESC)** button on the **Remote Assistance** window.
<u>On the helper's computer</u>: to stop controlling the other computer remotely, click the button Release Control .

G-Disconnecting the two computers

- From either computer, click the button (you may see a Disconnect or icon) to stop the connection with the other computer.
- Click **OK**.
- Close the **Remote Assistance** window by clicking its button.

5.6 Remote Desktop

A-Setting up Remote Desktop connection permissions

This chapter describes how to check the setup of the remote computer to which you want to connect, which must be running Windows XP Professional.

- Check that the **Allow users to connect remotely to this computer** option is active (**start - Control Panel - Performance and Maintenance - System - Remote** tab).

- Click the **Select Remote Users** button to create your personal permissions.

  Only administrators and authorised users can connect remotely.

- Click the **Add** button to add a new user account to which you wish to give remote connection permissions.

- In the **Enter the object names to select** box, give the name of the user concerned.

- Click the **Check Names** button so Windows can check the existence of the stated user.

- Click **OK** to confirm.

- Close all the windows by clicking **OK** on each one.

B-Defining/modifying connection settings on the second computer

The second computer, from which you will connect to the first, can use either Windows XP Professional or Home Edition. To work with other versions of Windows, (2000, Me, 98, 95), you will need to install the client application from the Windows XP CD-ROM (insert the CD-ROM, click **Perform additional tasks***, then click* **Set up Remote Desktop Connection** *and follow the instructions).*

- **start - All Programs** - **Accessories** - **Communications** - **Remote Desktop Connection**

- Click the **Options** button.

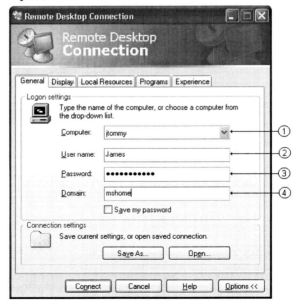

① Enter the name of the remote computer or its IP address (you can also click the arrow on the text box and click **Browse for more** to search for an available computer in the domain).

② Check the user name with which you will be logging on to the remote computer.

③ If you wish, enter your password.

④ If necessary, enter the workgroup or domain in which a session must be opened automatically.

▓ If you want to connect straightaway, click the **Connect** button. If you do this, the data you entered will be saved automatically in a file called **Default.rdp** and these will become the default settings for all Remote Desktop connections.

By default, .rdp files are saved as <u>hidden</u> files in the My Documents folder.

▓ If you want to save these settings under a particular name, click the **Save As** button.

Check that **Remote Desktop Files (*.RDP)** appears in the **Save as type** box and choose the required location before entering the **File name**, then click **Save**.

The other tabs (Display, Local Resources, Programs and Experience) contain options for changing the display settings of the remote computer, choosing local devices, starting certain applications when you start the remote session, optimising connection performance and so on.

⇨ *To modify the connection settings in an .rdp file, right-click the file and choose the Edit option.*

C-Using Remote Desktop Connection

▓ On the local computer, use: **start - All Programs - Accessories - Communications - Remote Desktop Connection**

▓ Enter the name of the **Computer** or IP address for the computer for which Remote Desktop has been activated and for which you have the appropriate permissions.

You can also click the arrow on the **Computer** text box and click **Browse for more** to search for an available computer in the domain.

The computer to which you wish to connect can be a Terminal Server or a computer using Windows XP Professional or Server.

▓ To define the connection settings, click the **Options** button and complete the text boxes as described in the previous section.

▓ Click the **Connect** button.

▓ In the **Log On to Windows** dialog box, enter your user name and password, then click **OK**.

The desktop of the remote computer appears, filling the entire screen (providing the remote computer is switched on and is connected to the Internet or its intranet). You can use the remote computer as if it were in front of you.

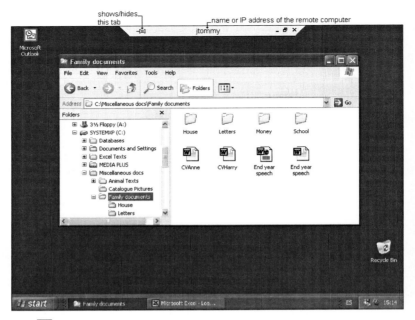

The [-] *button on the yellow tab at the top hides the Remote Desktop and returns you to your own desktop. To go back to the Remote Desktop, click the corresponding button on the taskbar.*

To disconnect, close the Remote Desktop window by clicking the [X] button on the yellow tab then confirm with **OK**.

Take note that this action does not close the session on the remote computer. Any open applications will keep working.

To close the session (and disconnect at the same time), click the **start** button, then choose **Log Off** and click the **Log Off** button.

Emoticons (for Windows Messenger)

To produce this icon	Type	To produce this icon	Type
☺	:-) or :)	🍸	(D) or (d)
☺	:-D or :d	☎	(T) or (t)
☺	:-O or :o	🐱	(@)
☺	:-P or :p	☕	(C) or (c)
☺	;-) or ;)	💡	(I) or (i)
☹	:-(or :(	☀	(H) or (h)
☺	:-S or :s	🌙	(S)
☺	:-| or :|	☆	(*)
👍	(Y) or (y)	♪	(8)
👎	(N) or (n)	✉	(E) or (e)
♥	(L) or (l)	👤	(M) or (m)
💔	(U) or (u)	🦇	:-[or :[
💋	(K) or (k)	🖐	(^)
🎁	(G) or (g)	☺	:'(
🌹	(F) or (f)	☺	:-@ or :@
👨	(X) or (x)		({)
🚶	(Z) or (z)		(})
📷	(P) or (p)		(W) or (w)
🎞	(B) or (b)		

A

ACCESSING

Other workstations on a network 128
Remote computer 143

ACCOUNT

See USER

APPLICATION

Adding to All Programs list 91
Installing 115
Leaving 7
Modifying/removing 116
Opening from Explorer 46
Starting 6

AUDIO CD

Adding tracks to
the Media Library 76
Copying music files to a CD 78
Copying music files to a portable
device 79
Downloading album information
from the Internet 71
Playing a specific track 70
Playing on the Media Player 70

B

BACKGROUND

Changing on desktop 96

C

CD

*See AUDIO CD, CD-ROM,
CD WRITER*

CD WRITER

Copying music to a CD 78
Managing files in copying queue 40
Preparing before copying 38
Writing files to CD-ROM 40

CD-ROM

Copying files to CD-ROM 40

CLIP

Adding to a project 62
Applying a transition 64
Changing properties 60
Modifying view 61
Moving/deleting/renaming 61
Previewing 65
Splitting 64
Trimming 63

CLOSING

Application 7
Turning off the computer 8
Window 11
Windows XP session 3

COLLECTION

Creating 60
Moving/deleting/remaining 61

COMPRESSING

See FILE COMPRESSION

COMPUTER

Connecting two computers
with Remote Desktop 143
Finding on a network 129
Shutting down 8

CONNECTION

Configuring a computer to use
remote assistance 131
Releasing control of a remote
computer 141
Using e-mail to establish
remote assistance 136
Using Messenger to establish
remote assistance 131

See also REMOTE ASSISTANCE

CONTACT

Adding a contact 120
Blocking/unblocking
communication 123
Calling for an audio/video
conversation 125
Deleting 123
Inviting to play a game 125
Replying to an invitation 127
Searching for a contact's details 122
Sending an instant message 123

See also REMOTE ASSISTANCE,
WINDOWS MESSENGER

COPYING

Clips in Movie Maker	61
Files/folders	37
Files/folders onto a CD-ROM	38
Music onto a CD	78

D

DATE

Changing the system date	101
Setting the date for a given region	102

DEFRAGMENT

Volume	106

DELETING

Clip/collection	61
Contact in Messenger	123
Custom toolbar	87
Desktop shortcut	94
File or folder	41
Files from Recycle Bin	42
List of recently used documents	91
Playlist (Media Player)	77
Removing an application	116
Scheduled task	112
Tips on file/folder deletion	42
User account	18
User password	14

DESKTOP

Changing background	96
Changing the system date/time	101
Cleaning up unused icons	104
Creating a shortcut	94
Creating custom theme	100
Description	4
Desktop objects	4
Managing icons	95
Reactivating deleted shortcuts	105
Using the Desktop Cleanup Wizard	104
Using the Start menu	4

DEVICE

Copying music files to a portable device	79
Digital signatures	112
Installing	112

DIALOG BOX

Defining appearance	97

DISK

Creating a password reset disk	15

See also DRIVE, FLOPPY DISK

DISPLAY

Icon display on the desktop	95
Screen colour/resolution	98
Window/dialog box	97

See also VIEW

DRIVE

Cleaning up	110
Renaming	53

See also VOLUME

DVD

Capturing a still image	74
Playing on the Media Player	72
Using extra tools	74

E

E-MAIL

Using to establish remote assistance	136
Using to send a movie	67
Using to send a picture	84
Using to send files/folders	46

EMOTICONS

Activating/deactivating	124

ENCRYPTION

Decrypting encrypted folders	21
Encrypting folders	20

EXPLORER BAR

Using	26

See also WINDOWS EXPLORER

INDEX

F

FAST USER SWITCHING

Activating/deactivating   19
Using   2

FAVORITES

Adding a Web page to Favorites   29
Organising the folder   29
Using the Favorites bar   29

FILE

Changing list presentation
in Explorer   32
Copying   37
Deleting   41
Deselecting   36
Finding with the Search
Companion   48
Importing into Movie Maker   58
Moving   41
Printing from the Explorer   45
Protecting/unprotecting   45
Renaming   41
Retrieving from Recycle Bin   42
Selecting   36
Sending by e-mail   46
Sending during remote
assistance   139
Sharing with other users   127
Using to open an application   46

FILE COMPRESSION

Compressed folders   44
Compressing in NTFS   43
Decompressing compressed
folders   44
Description   43

FIREWALL

Activating/deactivating   130

FLOPPY DISK

Formatting   52

FOLDER

Changing list presentation
in Explorer   32
Copying   37
Creating new   36
Deleting   41

Deselecting   36
Encrypting   20
Making private   19
Moving   41
Renaming   41
Selecting   36
Sending by e-mail   46
Setting folder view options   34
Setting up to contain pictures   82
Sharing with other users   127
Using personal folders   35
Using the Folders bar   27

FONT

Managing   104

FORMATTING

Floppy disk   52

G

GUEST

Activating/deactivating account   19

H

HARDWARE

See DEVICE, INSTALLING

HELP

Finding help on Windows   7
Saving/printing a help topic   7

HISTORY

Modifying display of history items   28
Searching in the History bar   28
Using the History bar   28

HOTMAIL

Setting up MSN account   22

See also WINDOWS MESSENGER

I

ICON

Managing on the desktop   95

IMPORTING

Files into Movie Maker   58

INDEXING

Searching with indexing   48

INSTALLING

Application   115
Device   112
System updates   117
Windows XP components   116

INSTANT MESSAGE

Sending an instant message   123
Sending to someone
who is not a contact   124

See also WINDOWS MESSENGER

INTERNET

Downloading album information   71
Searching with the Search
Companion   51-52

See also E-MAIL

L

LEAVING

See CLOSING

LOG ON

Logging off   3
With Fast User Switching   2
Without Fast User Switching   3

M

MEDIA

Using the Media bar   30

MEDIA LIBRARY

Adding CD tracks   76
Creating a playlist   77
Defining access rights   75
Description   75

MENU

Customising Start menu   89
Start menu   4

See also OPTION

MESSENGER

*See CONTACT, INSTANT
MESSAGE, WINDOWS
MESSENGER*

MOUSE

Defining how it is used   103

MOVIE

Saving in a file   65
Sending by e-mail   67
Sending to a Web server   67

*See also WINDOWS MEDIA
PLAYER, WINDOWS MOVIE
MAKER*

MOVING

Clips in Movie Maker   61
Files/folders   41
Taskbar   86
Tool on a toolbar   87
Toolbar   87
Window   10

MSN

Setting up MSN account   22

MULTIMEDIA

Using the Windows Media Player   69

*See also AUDIO CD, PICTURE,
SOUND, VIDEO, WINDOWS
MEDIA PLAYER, WINDOWS
MOVIE MAKER*

N

NET PASSPORT

Description   21
Setting up MSN account   22
Setting up with your e-mail
address   24

NETWORK

Accessing other workstations   128
Activating/deactivating a firewall   130
Creating a shortcut to a network
folder   128
Finding a network workstation   129
Going to a network place   128

INDEX

NUMBER

Setting regional number settings 102

O

OPENING

Application	6
Application from the Explorer	46
Messenger session	119
New work session	2
Project in Movie Maker	62
Windows Explorer	26
Windows Media Player	69
Windows XP	1

OPTION

Inserting into the start menu	91
Removing from start menu	93

See also MENU

P

PAINT

Creating Movie Maker title slides 59

PASSPORT

See NET PASSPORT

PASSWORD

Assigning to a user	12
Changing user password	14
Creating a password reset disk	15
Deleting user password	14
Remembering lost passwords	16

PERSONAL FOLDER

Description and location 35

PHOTO

See PICTURE

PICTURE

Preview in the Explorer	33
Printing	83
Sending by e-mail	84
Setting up a folder to contain pictures	82
Viewing	82
Viewing as a slide show	82

PLAYLIST

Creating in the Media Library	77
Deleting	77

PREVIEW

Clip/project in Movie Maker	65
Showing image preview	33

PRINTING

File from the Explorer	45
Installing a printer	115
Picture	83
System information	109

PROJECT

Adding a clip	62
Opening	62
Previewing	65
Saving	62
Using transition effects	64

PROPERTIES

Changing clip properties	60
Viewing system properties	54

PROTECTION

Activating/deactvating a firewall	130
Encrypting folders	20
Making folders private	19
Protecting/unprotecting files	45

R

RADIO

Adding a favorite station	79
Finding a radio station	79
Listening to Internet radio	79

RECORDING

From a digital camera	57
Narration	57
Source material	56

RECYCLE BIN

Emptying	42
Retrieving all contents	42
Retrieving one or more files	42
Viewing contents	42

REGIONAL OPTIONS

Setting regional date/number
options 102

REMOTE ASSISTANCE

Configuring before using 131
Connecting via Windows
Messenger 131, 136
Controlling another computer 140
Description 130
E-mailing a user to ask for help 136
Inviting a user to help you 132
Managing sent invitations 138
Releasing control 141
Replying to an invitation
via e-mail 137
Replying to an invitation
via Messenger 134
Sending a file 139
Supplying online advice 139
Viewing a friend's computer
screen 139

REMOTE DESKTOP

Connecting two computers 143
Modifying settings (second
computer) 142
Setting up permissions 141

RENAMING

Clip/collection 61
Drive 53
File or folder 41

RESTORE

See SYSTEM RESTORE

RETRIEVING

All the files in the Recycle Bin 42
One or more files from the
Recycle Bin 42

S

SAVING

Project in Movie Maker 62

SCHEDULED TASKS

Creating a task 111
Deactivating 112
Deleting a task 112
Modifying a task 111
Pausing tasks 112

SCREEN

Choosing a screen saver 96
Screen display settings 98
See also DISPLAY

SCREEN SAVER

See SCREEN

SEARCH COMPANION

Activate/desactivate a search
engine 51
Modifying preferences 47
Opening 47
Using to find people 52
Using to find Web pages 52
Using to search on your
computer/network 48

SEARCHING

For a computer on a network 129
For files/computers/people 48
For radio stations 79
For system data 109
Help with keywords 7
In the History bar 28
Internet with the Search
Companion 51
Using the Search bar 32

SELECTING

Deselecting files and folders 36
File/folder 36
Files to copy to CD-ROM 39

SHARING

File/folder with other users 127

SHORTCUT

Creating for a start menu item 94
Creating in a toolbar 88
Creating on the desktop 94
Creating to a network folder 128
Deleting from the desktop 94

SIZE

Resizing a window 10

INDEX

SOUND

Adjusting audio levels	65
Associating with an event	98
Recording a narration	57
Recording analogue sound material	56

SPLITTING

Movie Maker clip	64

START MENU

Adding option to All Programs list	91
Clearing list of recent documents	91
Customising	89
Description	4
Inserting an option	91
Removing options	93
Using	4

STARTING

See OPENING

SYSTEM

Displaying information	108
Installing system updates	117
Looking for system data	109
Printing system information	109
Viewing properties	54

SYSTEM RESTORE

Activating	107
Cancelling a system restoration	108
Creating a restore point	107
Restoring the system	107

SYSTEM TOOLS

Cleaning up a disk	110
Using system restore	107
Using the disk defragmenter	106
Using the task scheduler	110

T

TASKBAR

Description	4
Managing	86
Showing/hiding	86

THEME

Creating for the desktop	100

TIME

Changing the system time	101

TOOL

Moving on a toolbar	87

TOOLBAR

Creating a shortcut	88
Creating new/deleting	87
Moving	87
Moving a tool	87
Showing/hiding	87

TRACK

Adding to a playlist	77
Adding to the Media Library	76
Choosing to play a CD track	70

TRANSITION

Applying to Movie Maker clips	64
Managing	65

TRIMMING

Movie Maker clip	63

U

USER

Activating/deactivating Fast User Switching	19
Activating/deactivating Guest account	19
Adding new	12
Assigning password	12
Changing account type	18
Changing user name	17
Changing user password	14
Changing user picture	17
Deleting user account	18
Deleting user password	14

V

VIDEO

Playing DVDs	72
Recording analogue video material	56
Recording from a digital camera	57
Using the Media bar	30

VIEW

Changing look of Media Player 81
Folder list views in the Explorer 32
Modifying clip view 61
Seeing an image preview 33
Setting folder view options 34
Showing/hiding a toolbar 87
Showing/hiding the taskbar 86

See also DISPLAY

VOLUME

Defragmenting 106

W

WEB

Sending a movie to a Web server 67

WEB PAGE

Adding a Web page to Favorites 29

WINDOW

Changing size 10
Closing 11
Defining appearance 97
Description 9
Managing several windows 11
Moving 10

WINDOWS EXPLORER

Managing hierarchy
in Folders bar 27
Opening 26
Opening an application 46
Refreshing view 28

*See also DISPLAY, FILE, FOLDER,
SEARCHING*

WINDOWS MEDIA PLAYER

Changing appearance (skins) 81
Changing the visualization 70
Downloading album information 71
Opening 69
Using the Media Library 75
Using to listen to the radio 79
Using to play an audio CD 70
Using to play DVDs 72
Using to write CDs 78

See also AUDIO CD, TRACK

WINDOWS MESSENGER

Adding a contact 120
Calling another computer 125
Description 119
Inviting a contact for online
interaction 125
Replying to an invitation 127
Sending an instant message 123
Signing in 119
Using to establish remote
assistance 131

See also REMOTE ASSISTANCE

WINDOWS MOVIE MAKER

Creating a collection 60
Creating title slides in Paint 59
Description of the window 55
Importing a sound/video/
image file 58
Managing clips/collections 61
Recording source material 56
Saving movie in a file 65
Sending movie by e-mail 67
Sending movie to Web server 67

*See also CLIP, COLLECTION,
MOVIE, PROJECT*

WINDOWS XP

Description of the desktop 4
Installing system updates 117
Installing/uninstalling Windows
components 116
Logging off 3
Starting up 1
Using Help and Support Center 7

WORKSPACE

Description 4

Z

ZIP

Using compressed folders 44

See also FILE COMPRESSION

INDEX